The Scots Philosophical Monograph Series

While this monograph series is published on behalf of the Scots Philosophical Club, refereed by a panel of distinguished philosophers in the Club, and has as one of its aims the provision of a publishing outlet for philosophical work being done in Scotland, it is nevertheless international. The Club hopes to bring out original works, written in a lively and readable style, and devoted to central areas of current philosophical concern, from philosophers working anywhere in the world.

As a deliberate policy we have specified no areas of the subject on which the series is to concentrate. The emphasis is on originality rather than, say, on surveys of literature, commentaries on the work of others, or exegesis. Historical works will be included only in so far as they also contribute significantly to topical debates.

As well as our debt to the referees and consulting editors, we have to acknowledge a very real debt to the universities of Glasgow, Edinburgh, Aberdeen, Stirling and St Andrews who—despite the current stringencies—have given financial support to the series.

Executive Editors: Andrew Brennan, William Lyons

Consulting Editors:

Professors G H Bird *Stirling*
J R Cameron *Aberdeen*
Robin Downie *Glasgow*
Bernard Mayo *St Andrews*
A G Wernham *Aberdeen*
Crispin Wright *St Andrews*

Scots Philosophical Monographs Number One

THINGS THAT HAPPEN

Scots Philosophical Monographs

Scots Philosophical Monographs Number One

THINGS THAT HAPPEN
J E TILES

Series Editors *Andrew Brennan & William Lyons*

ABERDEEN UNIVERSITY PRESS

First published 1981
Aberdeen University Press
A member of the Pergamon Group

© J E Tiles 1981

British Library Cataloguing in Publication Data
Tiles, J E
Things that happen. — (Scots Philosophical; no. 1)
1. History — Philosophy
I. Title   II. Series
901   D16.8
ISBN 0-08-025724-0
ISSN 0144-3062

PRINTED IN GREAT BRITAIN AT
ABERDEEN UNIVERSITY PRESS

Contents

Acknowledgements

There are many people whose criticism and encouragement helped to bring this monograph to its present form. A less fully argued version of Section 1 appeared in *Analysis,* June 1976 and the present version retains several points which I was forced to sharpen under criticism from an anonymous referee. Susan Haack helped me to prune an inept piece of argumentation from Section 2. My colleagues at Reading, John Cottingham, Geoffrey Harrison, David Papineau, Michael Proudfoot and Liesl Osman enthusiastically discussed two different versions of the material in Section 5. The train of thought which eventually led to Section 8 was initiated by a remark about the individuation of a serving of ice cream made by Professor J. L. Ackrill in an Aristotle class in Oxford. The account of ideal boundaries attempted in that section received a great deal of sympathetic and stimulating attention from Professor M. A. E. Dummett.

An earlier version of much that appears here was included in a D.Phil. thesis submitted to Oxford University in 1978 and benefited from the criticisms of my examiners, Professor Sir Peter Strawson and Mr. Michael Woods. Their pressure to clarify the argument of Chapter 3 was reinforced by the referee appointed by the editors of this monograph series. In addition I am grateful for the help he gave me in shaping the final section.

Two people have assisted me through nearly the whole development of this monograph. Dr. A. J. Kenny, who supervised my D.Phil., time and again helped me to free myself from bogs of obscurity, pointed me in the direction of fruitful lines of thought, was patient with the slow way I often responded to guidance and was tolerant of the incredibly crude form my thought took at the outset of each new development. My greatest debt is to my wife, Mary, who not only had to endure many ill-tempered days when I was not making progress but who could appreciate my predicaments and experience the double frustration of having her suggestions for ways out of an impasse, which she never would have allowed herself to get into, rebuffed by a wilful husband who didn't want to do it *that* way. I was not always wilful. Many sections benefited from the fresh approach she would bring to what I was trying to do. (Sections

1 and 10 stand out particularly in this respect.) I do not think I could begin to repay her by dedicating this to her, but it is the least I can offer. So I hereby do.

Introduction

Things that happen are not, of course, *really* things are they? One cannot pack them in a suitcase, trip over them on the stairs, mix them in a bowl or bump into one twice in the space of an hour. If observations along these lines were all it took to settle the matter, there would not be any philosophical questions here.

If one were after sound legislation on how to use the word 'thing', it would be an opening worthy of philosophy to point out that the last of these observations (that one cannot bump into one twice in an hour) marks the important category of that which can be reidentified on the second of separate encounters. There might be point in carefully restricting the use of the word 'thing' to this category. It would still be possible to argue that such legislation would not disqualify events or happenings from the accolade of 'things' ('Are you still on the same operation you were on when I was in here last?'), but it rapidly becomes difficult to see what is at stake over the question whether events should be given the dignity of things.

The issues become less elusive if one is interested in the place within the logical structure of our thought of the variety of forms of reports we make about what happens. Fundamental to the structure logicians find in human discourse is the asymmetric form of the singular sentence.

> The basic combination in which general and singular terms find their contrasting roles is that of *predication*: 'Mama is a woman', or schematically '*a* is an *F*' where '*a*' represents a singular term and '*F*' a general term. Predication joins a general term and a singular term to form a sentence that is true or false according as the general term is true or false of the object, if any, to which the singular term refers.
>
> (Quine 1960 p. 96)

Happenings are, of course, reported by means of general terms such as 'coughed', 'blundered' and 'hit his sister'. Happenings also find their way into sentences via singular terms: 'Knott's fine catch', 'Harry's recent promotion', 'the explosion at the warehouse'.

Moves to regiment our language so that such occurrences of singular terms (as well as occurrences of apparent quantification over happenings) are reduced out, paraphrased away or assigned a derivative role might be said to amount to taking away from the things that happen all or some of the dignity of things. What is at stake here is at least clear; all these moves embody views about the logical structure of discourse.

In 1966 Donald Davidson sharpened the logical and metaphysical issues surrounding the notion of event by posing the question, 'Must a logical representation of the structure of our discourse quantify over events?' His answer was, yes, if it is to represent the pattern of adverbial modification (e.g. of English) and if it is to do justice to the phenomenon of event redescription. In the representation of the logical form of event and action reporting sentences, Davidson proposed to use the simple but powerful device of enlarging the domain of first order quantification to include events. To do this, he acknowledged, requires an account of the identity of events, and he proposed a criterion of event identity based on sameness of causes and effects.

Davidson's criterion, however, may be judged inadequate on several counts. Its weaknesses, as exposed in Section 1 of this monograph, are symptoms of a failure on Davidson's part to inquire how, and for what, a criterion of identity is to be used and how our grasp of criteria of identity for events relates to other aspects of our linguistic mastery. By means of these questions, the present monograph proposes further to sharpen the issues.

The attempts made here to answer these questions draw repeatedly on the work of P.F. Strawson. In *Individuals* he contended that a viable instrument of communication could do without concepts of particular events. Surveying Strawson's position, Davidson mistakes it for that of a reductionist; but Strawson does not maintain that the language we speak could be represented as free of concepts for (quantification over) events, but that communication—including reports of happenings—would not be impossible if our language were free of such concepts (quantification). While, if our discourse lacked concepts for (quantification over) other particulars, such as material bodies, communication *would* be impossible.

Strawson neglects to say what concepts for particular events do in (or for) our language, but Davidson's approach offers a ready answer: that a language with concepts of particular events (as well as particular states, conditions and processes) will have adverbial (predicate) modifiers; a language which lacks such concepts will not. Davidson's holist approach prevents him from asking whether, and with what effect, a part of language could function as an independent instrument of communication—questions which might enable us to discern elements of our own mastery of language. These would *not* be separate parts or stages of our *acquisition* of language, but rather distinguishable principles which are in fact mastered by a human child *en bloc,* but which when distinguished offer us insights into the logical structure of our language. Distinguishing them would involve imagining the situations of creatures who only partly reflect the purposes furthered and the abilities required when *we* communicate.

To bring what is evidently an ambitious programme under control, this monograph takes as its immediate objective the testing of part of Strawson's position set out two paragraphs above. Examining the idea that we could talk about happenings without concepts of event-particulars as a contention about our grasp of principles of identity for events involves a good measure of (sympathetic) reinterpretation of Strawson. The possession of concepts of event-particulars is taken here to involve an implicit grasp of principles of identity for events. It is far from clear that Strawson's account of the possession of such concepts would have amounted to the same thing (Section 3). Nevertheless the lines of attack to which the reconstructed position is open (Section 2) are very similar to those which Moravcsik used against the position as set out in *Individuals.* If one wishes to deny that a creature without a grasp of principles of identity for events could report happenings, one can (A) argue that the ability to report happenings (i.e. the use of verbs) requires such a grasp, (B) argue that without such a grasp some other essential aspects of communication (e.g. a grasp of Strawson's 'single unitary framework' of reference) would not be possible.

The reconstructed position can withstand the first line of attack. By re-examining and improving Strawson's account of a 'feature-placing language', Section 5 argues that the grasp of principles of identity may be separated from the ability to make appropriate responses to environmental situations (features). The feature placer has no principles of identity and so represents a total separation of these aspects of linguistic mastery. Strawson's position on the dispensablilty of event particulars points to the possibility of a similar separation between the grasp of how to use words to respond to events and the grasp of principles of identity for events—and this separation would be within the abilities of language users who possess principles of identity for such things as material bodies. The model presented by the feature placer also helps to bring home the point that the grasp of a principle of identity enables a language user to apply more than one word to a single thing.

In subsequent sections various principles are added to the feature placer's very limited mastery. The first step is to follow Strawson's suggestion that to possess concepts for particulars involves a grasp of their limits and extent. The logical theory of part and whole, mereology, is used to represent this grasp and to study the identity principle generated by treating this as a complete account. The model language user thus equipped is found to be still very limited and improvements are sought by adding elementary topological notions to mereology. The addition of topological notions suggests the importance of completeness, and further resources are sought by equipping the language user to impose 'marks'. Eventually a model language user is proposed who while far from reflecting everything in our grasp of identity principles, does at least reveal that the way in which Moravcsik proposed to mount the second line of attack will not succeed (Section 11).

Nevertheless, the reconstructed Strawsonian position is vulnerable to this line of attack. To mount it effectively requires considering a language user in a community of speakers all of whom have similar abilities, and asking what is required for such a community to have access to the single unified spatio-temporal framework of reference, which Strawson claimed was so vital. Because such a framework could be used to enable mobile creatures like ourselves to find their way around their environment, the constraints created by this use might easily cloud the issue. It can be argued (and is in Section 12) that creatures who can find their way about in a space of sufficient structure need a mastery of principles of identity for movements, but this is not a constraint arising strictly from the demands of communication. On the other hand, the Strawsonian position can be presented with a dilemma: either creatures who communicate require the ability to conceive of and talk about their own movements or it is possible for creatures who do not conceive of and discuss their own movements to communicate with each other without making use of principles of identity for events. But the former line is not open to someone occupying the Strawsonian position, since the argument of Section 12 shows such creatures require a grasp of principles of identity for events.

To close the other alternative requires considering a community whose members do not move and do not conceive of their own mobility. In order to treat their individual experiences as experiences of a single space, this immobile community would need to conceive of the movements of things from the purview of one member to that of any other. In order to do this they would not only need to be able to reidentify place-occupiers, but they would also need to redescribe the movements of those place-occupiers in terms of their parts. Being able to do so constitutes a grasp of a principle of identity for movements. In this way Strawson's position, that a unified spatio-temporal framework could be used without a grasp of principles of identity for events, is shown to be untenable.

The undermining of Strawson's position on events, while interesting in its own right, is used here as a vehicle to explore in what an understanding of identity principles consists. The final section draws together the lessons which can be learned from the models and arguments assembled in Sections 5-15.

1

The Identity of Things that Happen

Section 1

Davidson does not offer an adequate account of event identity.

Some English adverbs invite a representation in which they attach, like modal operators, to the whole sentence. 'Socrates was definitely wise', can, after all, be rewritten in English as 'It was definitely the case that Socrates was wise', but many adverbs resist this. 'Socrates died painlessly', cannot be rewritten as 'It was painlessly the case that Socrates died'.

Adverbs of the latter kind add complexity to the predicate term of a sentence (and will be referred to as 'predicate modifiers') which is difficult to represent in a first order canonical language. 'Died' and 'died painlessly' have to be represented by two distinct and structurally unrelated predicates. An English speaker immediately recognizes the validity of the statement represented as,

$$(x) (x \text{ died painlessly} \rightarrow x \text{ died})$$

but the canonical representation is effectively blind to this.

Davidson's device is to represent an event[1] reporting sentence as having one more place accessible to quantification than it appears to have. Thus 'Brutus killed Caesar,' contains not only the singular terms 'Brutus' and 'Caesar', but also reports the existence of an event, a killing, in which Brutus and Caesar participated as killer and killed. The sentence would be represented as

$$(\exists x)(x \text{ was a killing \& } x \text{ was of Caesar \& } x \text{ was by Brutus}).$$

What appear to be predicate modifiers are represented as predicates applying to this event. 'Socrates died painlessly' is represented

$$(\exists x)(x \text{ was a death \& } x \text{ was of Socrates \& } x \text{ was painless}).$$

Thus the entailment to 'Socrates died', represented,

$$(\exists x)(x \text{ was a death } \& x \text{ was of Socrates}),$$

is valid by elementary steps in predicate calculus.

Such a representation does not, as Davidson insists, require that the sentence represented have a singular term referring to the killing, for the sentence is represented as 'existential and general with respect to events' (1970 p. 221). Nevertheless quantified sentences in English such as 'Someone died painlessly' and 'Everyone admires Caesar' stand in a special semantic relationship to singular sentences such as 'Socrates died painlessly' and 'Brutus admires Caesar' (see Dummett 1973, pp. 17-18). Under Davidson's proposed analysis the sentence which would stand in the corresponding relationship to 'Brutus killed Caesar' would be 'The killing was of Caesar by Brutus'. This is, however uncommon and uncomfortable, a permissible English sentence.

Davidson represents not only adverbs as predicates, but also what linguists (e.g. Lyons 1968, pp. 364f.) call 'adjuncts', that is, pre-positional phrases which indicate time ('on the Ides of March'), location ('in the Forum'), instrument ('with a knife'), direction ('to Athens'), etc. The analysis thus offers a particularly elegant way of dealing with a phenomenon Kenny (1963 pp. 155-162) labeled 'variable polyadicity'. If predicate logic represents a verb as a relation, it is also effectively blind to the relationships that hold between

Caesar was killed,
Brutus killed Caesar,
Brutus killed Caesar with a knife in the Forum.

'It is,' Kenny noted, 'of the essence of any relation that its polyadicity [number of terms] should be stable' (p. 156), so each sentence must be represented by a distinct relation term. Davidson's device shows these sentences to be linked because they say more or less about a single event.

Clearly the viability of Davidson's analysis rests on the idea that one can say more than one thing about an event and this in turn on the idea that we can judge that the same event is being talked about. To support his analysis here, Davidson offers a general criterion of event identity. Without such a criterion the analysis does not immediately collapse, but it stands unsteady and exposed. The first task of this chapter is to remove the support Davidson's criterion offers to his analysis. The second task is to examine the pressures to which the proposed analysis is vulnerable once the support is removed.

Davidson's approach to event identity is to find a nexus of external relations (in this case based on the 'cause' relation) which provides, a 'comprehensive and continuously usable framework for the identification and description of events analogous in many ways to the space-time co-ordinate system for material objects.

(1970, p. 232)

The criterion is that two events are identical when they have exactly the same causes and effects. Where x and y are events,

$x = y$ if and only if $((z)$ $(z$ caused $x \leftrightarrow z$ caused $y)$ &
$((z)(x$ caused $z \leftrightarrow y$ caused $z))$.

(*ibid.* p. 231)[2]

Davidson evidently expects initial reaction to this to be that of dissatisfaction, for he hurries to point out that this is not *formally* circular, no identities appear on the right hand side of the bi-conditional. A proposed criterion, however, may be unusable for reasons other than formal circularity. The argument that Davidson's criterion is of no more value than if it had been formally circular will come in three stages.

(1) The criterion is not usable without a great deal of analytical work on the 'cause' relation.

(2) Given a plausible thesis about the 'cause' relation, the criterion is unusable even by a creature with perfect knowledge.

(3) It is unusable because we are uncertain what is to count as an event.

(1) Presenting identity criteria as definitions of the identity relation has a precedent in Frege's consideration of contextual definitions in *Grundlagen,* §§ 55-69. Although Frege ultimately rejected the use of such definitions, there are two respects in which it might be felt that such definitions are superior to that which Davidson offers. For example, Frege considers defining the concept, *the direction* of a line:

the direction of line a = the direction of line b
if and only if line a is parallel to line b.

Not only does the identity sign fail to appear on the right hand side of the bi-conditional, *neither* does a singular term or variable mentioning directions, *nor* a quantifier whose range includes directions. The right hand side of Davidson's definition mentions the events between which the identity relation is to be defined (i.e. x and y) and quantifies over a range which includes events.

If one specifies a real number by quantifying over real numbers (a domain including that number) one is said to have given an impredicative specification of that number. One need not share the misgivings of Russell and Poincaré about impredicative definitions to have misgivings about Davidson's definition, for he is doing something far more ambitious than attempting to specify a particular event by quantifying over a range including that event: he is offering a general criterion of identity for objects in the domain of events. If one requires the identity criterion for the objects of a domain to be fixed before quantifying over that domain, then Davidson does seem open to the charge of circularity.

In his own defence Davidson would point to the axiom of extensionality in set theory as the model of his proposed criterion (one of four models mentioned, 1970, p. 225):

$$x = y \text{ if and only if } (z)(z \in x \leftrightarrow z \in y).$$

Here both features which were sources of complaint in the previous paragraph are present, nevertheless the axiom is widely accepted as a definition of set identity. But in for example *ZF* set theory, this axiom is accompanied by a number of other axioms which supply a substantial part of the formal properties of the '$\in$' relation. Without similar axioms for the 'cause' relation Davidson has not finished the task of supplying a criterion of identity. It will be argued next that for epistemological reasons 'cause' is wholly unsuited to Davidson's requirements.

(2) Davidson denies he is claiming that 'the only way of establishing, or supporting, a claim that two events are identical is by giving causal evidence' (*ibid.,* p. 231). Nevertheless, he does hold it is a *sufficient* criterion,[3] which I take to be the claim that given two event descriptions it is always possible to determine on the basis of causal facts alone (given enough of them) whether they are of identical or distinct events.

But if we take into account a point made in a rough characterization of the 'analysis of singular causal statements hinted at' in another article by Davidson, we find ourselves caught in a circle which, however non-formal, seems thoroughly vicious:

> '*A* caused *B*' is true if and only if there are descriptions of *A* and *B* such that the sentence obtained by putting these descriptions for '*A*' and '*B*' in '*A* caused *B*' follows from a true causal law.
>
> (1968, p. 92n)

Our judgements about whether *A* caused *B* will, therefore, rest on judgements of the identity of events. For to redescribe *A* and *B*, say as *C* and *D* (where we have a causal law which yields '*C* caused *D*') is to judge *A* is identical to *C* and *B* identical to *D*.

If these latter judgements depend on whether *A* and *C*, *B* and *D*, have the same causes and effects, consider our position: In the absence of a true causal law yielding '*C* caused *B*', we are in no position to say whether *B* and *D* satisfy one condition of identity, namely having the same cause, *C*. Suppose we are fortunate enough to have such a law. Then an affirmative judgement that *A* is identical to *C* requires that *A* and C have the same effects. One effect of C is now known to be B, so we must determine if B is an effect of A. But this is precisely what we are trying to settle by determining whether A is identical to C.

Davidson (1970, pp. 224-5) shrugs off the suggestion that a criterion of identity must provide 'a general method for *telling*' when identity sentences are true. Such a method would have to include a method for deciding all sentences in the language, he argues, for if S is an arbitrary sentence and $(\imath x)(Fx)$ describes an event, then

$$(\imath x)(Fx) \ = \ (\imath x)(Fx \ \& \ S)$$

is a true identity sentence if and only if S is true.

> What we want, rather is a statement of necessary and sufficient conditions for identity of events, a satisfactory filling for the blank in:
> If x and y are events, then $x \ = \ y$ if and only if _____ .
> (1960, p. 225)

But why do we want such a thing? To justify speaking of events as objects or entities over which we may quantify. We succeed, Davidson agrees (*ibid.* pp. 216 & 224), if we can answer the question when sentences of the form '$x \ = \ y$' are true. To prove that we can answer such questions it is, to be sure, not necessary to provide an answer to all of them. But a criterion is, nevertheless, a standard by which to make judgements. If identity sentences had only the form $(\imath x)(Fx) \ = \ (\imath x)(Fx \ \& \ S)$ we could quickly finish the task by pointing out that the criterion for the truth of such sentences was simply that of the truth of sentence S. Of course, not all identity sentences have this form.

Whether we ought to be satisfied with Davidson's criterion will depend on whether and in what circumstances someone (perhaps only a creature with vastly superior knowledge and mental powers to our own) could *use* the criterion to settle identity questions. To use Davidson's criterion a creature must be able to determine the truth of causal statements without needing to redescribe events. He must, that is, be able to determine the truth of the sentences 'A is a cause of B' and 'C is a cause of B' without determining whether A is the same event as C. We must, therefore, imagine a creature who can survey an infinite number of such sentences and assign each a truth value in order to determine if all the effects of A are effects of C, and the causes of A are the causes of C.

There are two ways we might imagine this creature actually determining the truth of the required infinity of causal sentences. The first way would be by reference to causal laws, so that we have to imagine him as supplied with enough such laws to determine the truth of singular causal sentences whatever event descriptions they incorporate. As it would have to be possible to determine whether the last thing Henry did caused the explosion without identifying the last thing Henry did with his striking a match near a leaking gas pipe, we would need a law linking last acts and explosions. Superior mental capacities will, however, be of no avail; enough laws of this sort are simply not available.[4]

A second way of making the required causal judgements reflects what Davidson must have in mind: The creature is able to determine directly, without the mediation of a causal law, an objective causal relation.

> Causality and identity are relations between individual events no matter how described. But laws are linguistic; and so events can instantiate laws, and hence be explained or predicted in the light of laws, only as those events are described in one or another way.
>
> (1971, p. 89; cf. 1976 b, p. 697 & *passim*.)

Such a judgement, however, would require acquaintance with events A, B and C which took no account of the desriptions under which they fell, and a creature able to make such judgements could not fail to recognize whether the question, 'Is A a cause of B?' was distinct from the question, 'Is C a cause of B?' The questions could only be distinct questions requiring distinct judgement if the events A and C were distinct. A creature only needs to make identity judgements if his other judgements must take account of the descriptions under which objects fall. A creature able to perceive causal relations directly could use Davidson's criterion, but would have no *need* to use it.

(3) The problem of (2) is faced only by a creature who has recognized 'A', 'C', etc. as event descriptions. it may not be the aim of Davidson's criterion to enable us to settle what is to count as an event description, but the criterion is useless we are able to settle such questions. Consider again the model that the extensionality axiom provides. In ZF set theory this axiom has the effect of restricting the universe of the theory so that only one object—the empty set—is memberless. To create a more familiar kind of set theory out of ZF, one has to restrict the variables x and y of the axiom to sets and allow the variable z to range more widely. In this case the axiom relies on the criteria of identity of those objects in the range of z which are not sets. As Davidson does not *say* that z ranges only over events, we *may* be supposed to take his criterion to function in this way.

One would not be inclined to regard everything that can enter the 'cause' relation as an event. States are said to be causes (the car skidded because the tyres were worn) and to be effects (the tyres were worn by 100,000 miles of travel). Are states to be considered as events their identity criterion given by Davidson's formula, or do they require a separate account? People are said to be causes. Are we to go so far as to count people as events? Clearly we have to know what else is in the range of the variable z, and how to distinguish these other objects from events if we are able to use Davidson's criterion.

A quick answer to these questions would be to rule that an event description is anything that lies in the range of significance of the 'cause' relation. That this range includes descriptions of states should present no problem, if Davidson is prepared to go part way with those philosophers (see van Fraassen 1970, p. 32 and Broad 1923, pp. 54-5) who regard states as paradigm events. This quick answer, however, confronts Davidson with an uncomfortable extension of the scope of his proposed analysis, for no tensed sentences will escape the additional quantifier which Davidson says an event sentence requires in its representation. Davidson does not suggest, either explicitly or implicitly by his choice of examples, that every tensed sentence (e.g. 'The tyres were worn') requires the additional quantifier.[5] It is here the failings of his identity criterion leave his analysis of event sentences most exposed, for as our unclarity tempts us to apply the analysis more and more widely we encounter pressures which threaten to sweep the whole proposal away. Those temptations and pressures will be examined next.

Section 2

Strawson's thesis about the conceptual dependence of event particulars can withstand certain criticisms if sympathetically reinterpreted. The reinterpreted thesis is open to attack along two lines (to be pursued in Chapters 2 and 3).

Strawson's discussion (1963, pp. 168-182) of what transformational grammarians call 'nominalization' reveals the source of the temptation to extend Davidson's analysis beyond what was intended. Nominalization is a transformation which embeds a sentence into a more complex sentence by first turning it into a noun phrase. Thus 'Socrates died' is nominalized to produce 'Socrates' death', and this noun phrase may appear as a singular term in a sentence such as,

Socrates' death failed to shame the citizens of Athens

Sentences such as 'Carr caught Compton out' and 'Peter struck John' nominalize respectively to 'The catch Carr made which got Compton out' and 'The blow Peter gave John'. Clearly this is the grammatical source of many singular terms which refer to events.

Nominalizations take adjectival modifiers where the corresponding verbs take adverbial modifiers:

Carr skillfully caught Compton out,
Carr's catch was skillful;

Socrates died painlessly
Socrates' death was painless.

This much harmonizes with Davidson's approach to such an extent that to indicate his position we merely have to add that in his view the second of each of these pairs has a surface grammar which more accurately reflects its true logical form.

Strawson, however, does not regard nominalization as restricted to producing event singular terms. He discusses the phenomenon in terms of his distinction between sortal and characterizing universals. If rather than to universals, we apply the distinction to general terms then a 'sortal general term' would be one whose mastery 'of itself provides a principle for distinguishing, enumerating and reidentifying particulars of a sort,' (1963, p. 220), while a 'characterizing general term' would be one the mastery of which puts a speaker in a position to group and count 'particulars already distinguished or distinguishable, in accordance with some antecedent principle or method' (*ibid.* p. 168). Verbs, according to

Strawson, are characterizing general terms undistinguished in any respect important for his discussion.

As nominalization is not confined to verbs, 'Socrates was wise' can be nominalized to produce

> The wisdom of Socrates (is preserved for us by Plato),

and 'Ted was angry' to

> Ted's anger (cooled rapidly).

Such nominalizations also attract adjective modifiers which correspond to adverb modifiers in the sentence to be nominalized (hereafter the 'underlying sentence').

> Ted was intensely and violently angry.
> (Ted's anger was intense and violent.)
>
> Socrates was profoundly wise.
> (Socrates' wisdom was profound.)
>
> He was hideously pale.
> (His pallor was hideous.)
>
> Her outfit was aggressively masculine.
> (The masculinity of her outfit was aggressive.)

If Davidson's analysis works when the adverb attaches to a verb such as 'killed', 'strolled', 'buttered (the toast)', why should we refrain from applying it to these four examples? But while Davidson might be content to treat Ted's (spell of) anger as an event, Socrates' wisdom, particular skin conditions and particular masculinities of feminine outfits are not only unlikely events, they will be difficult to sell as respectable objects to those philosophers who are sensitive about what they include in the domain of their quantifiers.

To avoid the uncontrolled proliferation of objects resulting from such nominalizations, we might insist that where the same thought can be expressed without the noun phrase, we need not recognize the entity to which the phrase purports to refer. It is easy to find replacement sentences for those sentences which we would ordinarily think of as reporting causal relations, for example:

> The platoon commander's lack of a map of the area was fatal to the operation.

One does not need to treat 'the platoon commander's lack of a map of the area' as referring to an entity, Dummett (1973, pp. 70-72) argues, for this is just another way of saying

The operation failed because the platoon commander had no map of the area.

A reductionist could apply this strategy widely and might press against Davidson the thesis that 'cause' primarily links sentences, not singular terms.

As to those pairs of sentences, one of which uses an adverb, the other of which applies an adjective to the result of nominalization, the reductionist would insist that the former shows us we can dispense with the latter. Davidson can meet this pressure by pointing to the success of his analysis. But unless Davidson can show us how to limit the scope of his analysis by saying what does and what does not count as an event, the reductionist will find the price of an uncomfortably inclusive domain of quantification too high pay for the felicities of Davidson's analysis (that is, assuming he is prepared to tolerate events of any kind).

Strawson uses his discussion of nominalization to support neither a position favourable to Davidson nor the pressure to reduce or eliminate sentences involving reference to events. Strawson's thesis is phrased in terms of the key notions, 'propositional tie' and 'dependence'. Whenever a characterizing universal, e.g. *dying*, is linked to a particular like Socrates,

> . . . we can frame the idea of another particular bound to the first by the attributive tie; so to the characterizing tie between Socrates and the universal, *dying*, there corresponds the attributive tie between Socrates and the particular, his death.
>
> (1965, p. 170)

As a result of this 'framing of the idea of another particular', adverbs are seen to introduce characterising universals which are collected by this new particular. There is some indication that the procedure may be iterated (Cf. p. 172, n. 18), framing a further particular from the adverbially introduced universal which will be subject to further characterization. Strawson's remarks, thus can be illustrated by Figure 1.

Strawson writes of 'ties' here because Socrates and Socrates' death are not particulars of the same logical status, and thus are not linked by a relation. In this respect Strawson's position differs importantly from Davidson's: for Davidson the two have the same logical status and are linked by an ordinary first order two place predicate. Strawson expresses the different status of Socrates' death in terms of 'dependence': Every attributive tie links a (relatively) dependent member and a (relatively) independent member. The independent member, e.g. Socrates, can 'collect' many characterizing universals and thereby many particulars

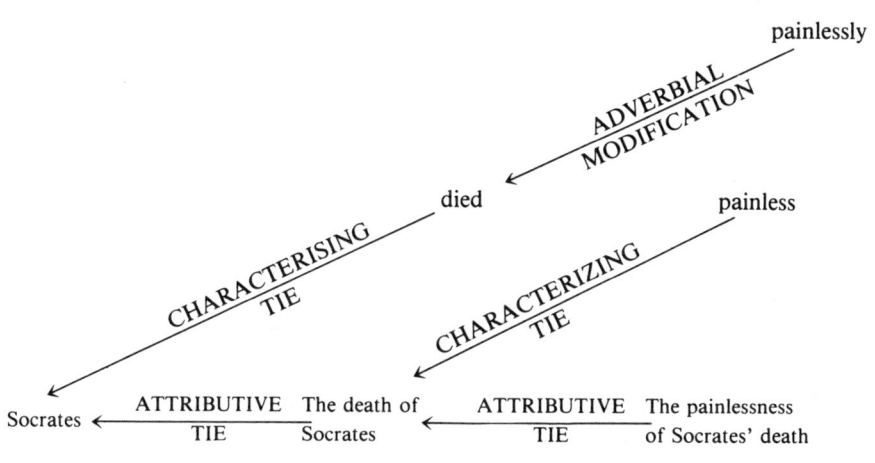

Figure 1

'similar to' Socrates' death. The dependent member can 'collect' only one particular 'similar to' the independent member (1963, p. 172). This sets up an asymmetry, but does not vividly express, what is clearly on Strawson's mind, that it is the identity and individuality of the dependent member which depends on that of the independent member.

In Chapter I (1963, pp. 41-3) Strawson argues for the conceptual dependence of one class of dependent particulars, events, on a class of independent particulars, material bodies. As Davidson says:

> [Strawson's] principal argument may, I think be not unfairly stated as follows: in a sentence like 'There is an event that is the birth of this animal' we refer to, or quantify over, events and objects alike. But we can, if we please, express exactly the same idea by saying 'This animal was born' and here there is no reference to, or quantification over, events. We cannot in the same way eliminate the reference to the object.
>
> (1970, p. 226)

This, Davidson replies, proves too much or too little. If the sentences are equivalent then if the second requires no event, neither does the first. If, on the other hand, the first requires an event, so does the second.

Davidson takes Strawson's argument to be based on the reductionist's strategy, but Strawson is not advancing the reductionist's position, nor *can* his argument be based on this strategy. His argument ('as finally amended') does not appeal to the fact that two such sentences may 'express exactly the same idea'. It appeals rather to the principle that we could not have a concept of a birth without the concept of particular animals who are born, but we could have the concept of an animal if we only spoke of animals as *being born* and made no use of the concept of a *particular birth*. If the sentences, 'There is an event which is the birth of this animal' and 'This animal was born' express *exactly the same idea, how can* Strawson suggest we could use the latter without having a concept of a particular birth?

Strawson may simply be wrong about the difference between sentences such as these, and a point which Davidson could press is that Strawson has failed to tell us what the difference is. If we 'find a place in our discourse for the idea of a certain range of particulars, viz. births' (1963, p. 42), what have we added apart from another way of expressing what we can already say?

Although Strawson does not, he *might* appeal to the very phenomenon which motivates Davidson's analysis, viz. adverb and adjunct modification. The basis of the reply to the question of the previous paragraph, which I am about to construct for Strawson, is laid in another context, (1971, pp. 65-74) where Strawson observes that nothing stands in the way of treating the substantives 'prettiness', 'wit', and 'willingness' as singular terms, because as 'pretty' collects together young ladies such as Betty and Sally, 'qualities desirable in a date' collects together the like of prettiness and willingness. Quantification over such abstract particulars is likewise justified. Moreover, quantification (and, one may suppose, treating abstract singular terms seriously) only has a point because such collection principles are at hand.

> In general it will never be to the purpose to quantify over items of a higher type unless some still higher-type principle of collection is being implicitly used.
>
> (1971, p. 73)

The fact that adverbs, e.g. 'painlessly', supply principles which collect, e.g. 'Socrates died', and 'His father removed the sliver', is sufficient for there to be a point to attributive particular quantification. A nominalization transformation is not necessary, but something which invites representation as predicate modification, some form of collection of particular applications of general terms, is necessary to give such quantification a point.

The answer to the question, 'What do we add when we "find a place in our discourse for the idea of a certain range of particulars"?' will be 'principles which collect such particulars permitting them to be characterized' and in the case under discussion, 'principles which collect particular applications of general terms'. (An improvement to this answer is suggested at the end of Section 5.) In English the mastery of these principles can be displayed either by applying adjectives to attributive singular terms or by applying adverbs to general terms.

However, there is no reason why a language has to be equipped to modify predicates. Strawson could agree that 'This animal was born,' and 'There is an event which is the birth of this animal' have the same truth conditions, but insist that the difference between them is that the form of the first allows it to belong to a predicate-modifier-free language, while the form of the second indicates that it belongs to a language with predicate modifiers.

By swelling the domain of first order quantification, Davidson represents the role of adverbs in English as ordinary first order predicates. This, Strawson might contend, obscures rather than explains (gives an adequate theoretical representation of) our linguistic mastery. For one thing, Davidson represents an English speaker's mastery of 'This animal was born', 'Socrates died', etc. as involving a grasp of principles for collecting the likes of births and deaths. An English speaker *does* possess such principles, but does not *need* to employ them in order to use such sentences. A Davidsonian analysis may reflect the connection which such sentences have to other parts of English, but it obscures the fact that a portion of English—an adverb-free fragment—could exist as an independent (if less expressive) instrument of communication. More importantly, the representation of the grasp of principles for collecting the likes of births and deaths by an increase in the domain of first order quantification—so that births and deaths stand shoulder to shoulder with men and animals—obscures the fact (as Strawson sees it) that one could not have a grasp of principles for collecting the likes of births and deaths unless one possessed principles for collecting the likes of men and animals.

This parry and riposte to Davidson's attack on Strawson's thesis can also be used in reply to Davidson's suggestion that the dependence of events on particular substances (material bodies) is part of a reciprocal conceptual dependence:

Substances owe their special importance in the enterprise of identification to the fact that they survive through time. But the idea of survival is inseparable from the idea of surviving certain sorts of change—of position, size, shape, color, and so forth.

(1970, p. 227)

As Davidson acknowledges (1973, n. 14) Moravcsik makes a similar point:

> At one place Strawson argues that events such as strikes can not be basic particulars, for we could not have the concept of a strike without having such concepts as those of tools and factories. To this, however, it should be replied that neither could we have the concepts of tools and factories without having such concepts as those of production, manufacturing, &c.
>
> (1968, p. 117)

Strawson could agree that we could not have the idea of a tool unless we applied the verbs 'produce', 'manufacture', etc., but deny that this requires 'framing the idea' of particular productions to which modifiers can be attached. The reciprocal dependence of particulars on the universals they collect does not establish a reciprocal dependence between dependent and independent particulars.

But even when reinforced in the way here suggested, Strawson's position appears vulnerable if either one of two theses can be made out. (a) To possess concepts of the paradigm independent particulars, material bodies, requires not only applying verbs, but also 'framing ideas' of particular events.
(b) One cannot master the application of verbs (on which, it has been admitted, the possession of the concepts of particular material bodies depends) unless one 'frames ideas' of particular events. Moravcsik locates both of these targets. The second he does not pursue farther than to say,

> If we could not count and refer to births, the meaning of '_____ is born' would be different from what it is; . . . (1968, p. 118)

Most certainly it would, but so different that we would be justified in saying that a person unable to count and refer to births is not master of the general term '_____ is born'? This line of attack will be taken up and pursued in Sections 4 and 5 below.

To understand how the first thesis can be pressed against Strawson's position we need a clearer picture of that position. There is an obvious way in which the identity of some events would have to depend on the identity of 'material bodies', (e.g. the identity of the change in a body depends on the identity of that body). Strawson does not maintain that all of what we might describe as events are so dependent. He mentions a class of 'events or processes' which are not necessarily conceived by us as,

> . . . *of* or performed or undergone *by* material bodies . . . that a flash or bang occurred does not entail anything flashed or banged.
>
> (1963, p. 36)

Nothing prevents such events from being regarded as *independent particulars*.

There is a further thesis that events, even of this independent variety cannot constitute the only class of particulars in a language user's conceptual scheme. They cannot do so because they cannot provide for the requirements of communication, in particualr for the need to refer identifyingly. This thesis Strawson expresses by saying that events are not *basic particulars*. What Strawson calls 'material bodies' do, on the other hand, provide for the requirements of communication and can do so even if the language does not contain concepts for other particulars such as events. Concepts for 'material bodies' fulfil a role in our language which, Strawson insists, must be fulfilled, but his argument (by his own admission, 1963, pp. 29-30) establishes at most the need for spatial continuants which are not necessarily what we would think of as 'material' (We might make do with 'purely visual three dimensional objects' p. 30.) In any case the basic particulars succeed in providing what Strawson sees as a requisite of communication because they can be organized in a 'common and continuously extendable framework of reference' (1963, p. 44).

It is against this position that the first thesis may be developed, for the framework is said to be constituted by both spatial and temporal relations. Are not temporal relations first and foremost relations between *events*? If basic particulars depend on temporal relations and temporal relations depend on events, how can Strawson maintain the position outlined above on his behalf? Strawson's brief treatment of this objection does not address itself to the crucial points,

> The fact that identification in general has a temporal as well as a spatial aspect is no objection. For material bodies, or things which have them, exhibit relations between themselves which have a temporal aspect.

> (1963, p. 45)

But can we temporally relate bodies without doing so via the events in which they participate? Can these relations which exhibit a 'temporal aspect' be grasped without an ability to identify particular events of the kind Strawson would classify as dependent?

Moravcsik's attack on Strawson via the first thesis also turns on the question of whether we would have the necessary temporal concepts without a grasp of the identity of events. He argues for the first thesis by contending that *reidentification* of a material body would be impossible unless we could,

> locate two segments of time which the body allegedly occupied and occupies. I do not see how such locating would be possible without reference to events, or times . . . If we attempt to locate these time segments

by reference to other bodies only, we shall not be able to relate them to the observer, and this is surely crucial for reidentification. Furthermore, reference to times presupposes some reference to events.

(1968, p. 116)

To see whether the reinforced Strawsonian position which has been set out here is vulnerable to an attack of this kind, a fairly detailed account of the grasp of the identity of times and particular events will have to be set out. The work for this will be done in Sections 6 to 10 and we will not be in a position to evaluate the force of this attack until the end of Section 11. For the remainder of this chapter, Strawson's postion as outlined above will be disentangled from a further and unsupportable thesis about the grasp of the identity of events, and then more will be said about the second thesis which might be pressed against Strawson's position.

Section 3
The grasp of the identity of events cannot be accounted for simply by listing the semantically significant parts of a sentence reporting that event.

A reductionist, unwilling to countenance events at any price, has nothing to offer in place of Davidson's analysis of adverbial modification except a feeling of ontological purity. Strawson, on the other hand, is in a position to preserve the felicities of Davidson's analysis, for he uses the same schema—applying a general term to a singular term—to represent adverbial modification. The difference is that for Strawson the singular terms which collect such general terms (and associated quantification) must be sharply distinguished from other singular terms (and quantification). Is there any way to provide a theoretical representation of Strawson's position?

Following R. M. Martin and B. M. Taylor, we might represent what has here been called a 'dependent particular' by an ordered n-tuple of the semantic elements required for giving the truth conditions of the underlying sentences. The semantic elements required are (1) the objects referred to by the singular terms, (2) something to represent the general term, either its extension (treated as a set or as a virtual class) or something sophisticated such as a function on possible worlds. These elements are then arranged in ordered n-tuples, where the order of the objects may be used to reflect how they stand in asymmetrical relations. The blow Peter gave John would be represented by

$$< \text{strike, Peter, John} >$$

and John's retaliation by

$$< \text{strike, John, Peter} >,$$

Socrates' death by

$$< \text{die, Socrates} >$$

and Socrates' wisdom by

$$< \text{wise, Socrates} >.$$

The spirit in which this analysis is offered may be expressed thus: Davidson's events are obscure and we cannot claim to understand what they are. Ordered n-tuples of elements, already needed for the semantic account of simpler sentences, offer a ready explication of the vital but obscure notion and afford a significant broadening and deepening of

Davidson's analysis. His analysis is extended because it will cope with adverbs which we do not ordinarily think of as modifying event expressions (e.g. 'x is profoundly wise'). His analysis is strengthened because it can be made to reflect our feeling that when Davidson represents 'Someone killed Caesar' by,

$$(\ x)(\ y)(x \text{ is a killing } \& \ x \text{ was by } y \ \& \ x \text{ was of Caesar}),$$

something should be done to suggest that Caesar's killing is quite a different sort of thing from Caesar's killer. This can be done by a special style of letter, Greek or Gothic instead of Roman, for event quantification, but this only emphasizes the difference and does nothing to explain it. If event quantifiers range over ordered sets of objects and other quantifiers over objects, then we have something for a change in the style of letter to reflect. Taylor 1974, accordingly, contains an elaboration of a Tarski semantics to accommodate this suggestion.

Although both Taylor and Martin hoped to explain what is unclear (fact, events, states of affairs) in terms of what they regarded as clear (objects, classes of objects, periods and instants of time) and did not aim to give a theoretical representation of a language user's mastery of a portion of his native language, it is, nevertheless, possible to evaluate their suggestion as a contribution to this latter aim. We cannot, of course, treat a language user as literally predicating adverbs and adjuncts of ordered n-tuples of semantic elements, but we can take the approach as embodying two important theses about the user's grasp, both of which seem to reflect Strawson's attitude in *Individuals*:

Thesis (1) The grasp of the underlying sentence, and hence of its semantically significant parts, is a necessary condition of being able to 'frame the idea' of a dependent particular (event, fact, state of affairs), but one need not 'frame the idea' of any further dependent particular and apply general terms to it in order to grasp the underlying sentence.
Thesis (2) The grasp of the *identity* of the further particular may, nevertheless, be accounted for by a list representing the grasp of those semantically significant parts, for nothing more is required for a language user to go ahead and 'frame the idea' of the further particular and apply characterizing general terms to it.[6]

I think this approach and the theses I have taken it to embody can be evaluated without exploring the subtleties which occupy either Martin or Taylor, but there is one obvious flaw in the rough sketch I have presented of their approach to event analysis which cannot be overlooked. Peter may (viciously) strike John more than once; Mary may (painstakingly) pitch the same tent more than once in the same place. Which blow or tent pitching do '<strike, Peter, John>' and '<pitch, Mary, the tent>' represent? To accommodate these differences we must follow Martin and Taylor in enlarging the list of semantic elements to include the *times* when Peter struck John and Mary pitched the tent. Thus one tent pitching is represented by '<pitch, Mary, the tent, 5.00-5.30 p.m. 29/8/80>'. The blows Peter inflicted on John may be separated only by seconds but each landed at a different instant, thus '<strike, Peter, John, t_1>' is distinct from '<strike, Peter, John, t_2>'.

This amendment does not require abandoning or modifying either the theses mentioned above. Tense is a semantically relevent part of the underlying sentence and the list of semantic elements used hitherto is simply incomplete. This device, however, treats the grasp of the tense of a sentence as analogous to the referring role of other parts of the sentence. As with Davidson's analysis, it represents apparent n-place relations in the natural language by $n+1$-place relations, adding in this case an additional place for a 'time'. But if the grasp of tense is to be represented by a period or instant referred to (directly or indirectly) by the underlying sentence, something will have to be done to elucidate our command of the identity criteria of such 'times'.

A quick survey of the prospects suggests it will be difficult to account for this grasp without a prior account of our grasp of event identity. One cannot say how long a period of time is without mention of some standard event the duration of which is some multiple or fraction of that event. (A similar point threatens Strawson.) One cannot locate instants or periods except by locating them in a framework of events in which the act of mentioning a period or instant can itself be located. An account of the mastery of this additional item in the ordered n-tuple may in the end bring us full circle and undermine the point of this style of event analysis.[7]

If we set the problem with 'times' to one side we will still have to reckon with the chief complaint that Davidson (1970, p. 222-3) levels at this style of event analysis, which is that it makes it impossible to see how we can identify an event under different descriptions. Under the analysis we are considering we cannot even say that Brutus' murder of Caesar was Brutus' killing of Caesar. The difficulty arises if we represent general terms by objects which are distinct if the applications of the terms differ.

This will be the case for almost any available object we choose for our general term, whether it be the extension of the term or a function on possible worlds. If the objects representing the general terms 'kill' and 'murder' are distinct (because some killings are not murders), then the objects which serve as the referents of 'Brutus' killing of Caesar' and 'Brutus' murder of Caesar' will be distinct. But if it is true to say Brutus murdered Caesar, it would seem wrong to say this was a distinct event from his killing Caesar.

This presents a serious difficulty for the Martin-Taylor analysis of events only if we are in fact able to identify the same event under different descriptions. Davidson here creates difficulties for his own position by an occasional choice of problematic examples. He would like, for example, to maintain that Brutus' stabbing Caesar was the same event as his killing Caesar. This is plausible if our thinking is governed by the question, 'What did Brutus do?' He stabbed Caesar; he did not then have to do something else which was killing Caesar. But there is a problem if Caesar takes a long time to die from his wound. During this time it is true and natural to say that Brutus has stabbed Caesar, but not that Brutus has killed Caesar. The latter does not become natural and obviously true until Caesar dies from his stab wound. (See Thompson 1971.)

Davidson holds that if Caesar does eventually die from his wound, then it is true (although admittedly not natural, because we are not yet aware of this truth) to say Brutus has killed Caesar at any time after he has stabbed Caesar and before Caesar dies:

> To describe an event as a killing is to describe it as an event (here an action) that caused a death and we are not apt to describe an action as one that caused a death until the death occurs; yet it may be such an action before the death occurs.
>
> (1970, p. 229)

To describe an event as a killing may, however, not be to describe it as *causing* a death. The death might be *part of* what is described. (A suggestion similar to this is made by Thalberg 1971, pp. 786-7.)

Some events are, after all, complexes of events. This is true of complex actions such as making bread, and even of fairly simple happenings. Reporting on a tedious hour spent alone in a room, a person might say that only one thing happened, a light bulb flickered out briefly, but even this one event is a complex of two changes in the light bulb, on to off and off to on. If a case can be made for regarding a killing as a complex of two events, a stabbing and a death, then Davidson has made unnecessary trouble for himself by confusing a part of an event with the whole of that event.[8] It is as though he took a pair of glasses to be identical to a pair of lenses, forgetting about the frames (Thalberg's example).

If this were an obvious mistake Davidson would not have made it.[9] It is natural to allow our thinking to be governed by the question, 'What did Brutus do?' and difficult to accept that one of the things he is said to have done, kill Caesar, is composed of two events, only one of which was something Brutus is said to have done, stab Caesar, while the other was not Brutus' action at all. The difficulty is aggravated by the consequence that should Caesar linger mortally wounded it may take significantly longer to kill him than to stab him. It is, however, possible to come to terms with this consequence and the analysis of 'kill' is thereby made easier to accept.

The reason we hesitate to say a killing took longer than a stabbing is that the questions 'How long does (did) it take to ϕ?' are not always univocal, (particularly where 'ϕ' is a performance verb—Kenny 1963). The question, 'How long does it take to make bread?' may be after the length of time between taking out the flour and yeast to the point where the bread comes out of the oven, or it may be after how much bread making takes out of one's time for doing other things. If one is interested in the latter question, bread making will be thought of as exhausted by the actions of mixing, kneeding, setting to rise and putting in the oven. But as in the case of assassination, after performing the constituent actions, one has to let nature take its course.

In one perfectly good sense a person has not made the bread until it comes out of the oven, even though there is nothing he has to do while it bakes; he has not killed a man until that man dies; he has not grown a marrow until the seed he planted grows into a plant which bears fruit.[10] The endpoint determined by a verb of production is the realization of the product.

Far from casting doubt on Davidson's contention that events can be redescribed, the possibility of saying one event is a complex of events requires his contention to be true. There are, moreover, cases of identifying under different descriptions where there is no question of event complexity. If Brutus murdered Caesar, his murder was the same event as his killing Caesar; nothing needs to happen for the murder to become the killing or the killing (providing it satisfies the legal requirements) to become the murder. During an afternoon's bridge the first time I play a club may be the only time I trump my partner's trick. The last time I closed the front door may have been the first time I locked myself out of my present address. The throwing of the cargo of tea into Boston Harbour is the most renowned of the protests by the American colonists against Parliamentary Taxation. The movement of the body $\sqrt{2}$ miles NE will be its movement (approximately) one mile closer to the North Pole.

Such examples threaten the second thesis embodied in the Martin-Taylor approach, for it appears now that our grasp of the identity criteria of at least some attributive particulars, facts, or states of affairs, cannot be exhaustively represented by our grasp of the semantically

relevant parts of the underlying sentence. The source of this thesis was
the observation that one could report a protest, a blunder, or a trumping
of a trick by a sentence without the substantive or gerund construction,
e.g.,

> They protested about unfair taxation,
> I locked myself out of the house,
> I trumped the trick.

But the sentences

> They threw a cargo of tea into Boston Harbour,
> I closed the front door,
> I played a club,

may be taken to report in each case the same something or other (which it
is natural to call an 'event') and any account which relies only on the
truth conditions of the sentences in each pair will in no way reflect the
grasp of this possibility.

It is not in order for the defender of the Martin-Taylor analysis to
shrug off the distinction it creates between my playing a club and my
trumping my partner's trick, by declaring there simply are two events
where we thought there was only one. To ignore the pressure to say that
we *can* tell when two sentences report one event and when they report
two events is to assume there can be no criterion of event identity apart
from what the analysis determines.

There are two ways the ordered set analysis might try to do justice to
the phenomenon of redescription. One is suggested by Taylor's response
to the problem. Realizing that his analysis does not 'sanction' all the
substitutions *salve veritate* of event descriptions which ordinary language
does, Taylor decides these additional substitutions are made on the basis
of a looser relation which he calls 'kinship'. ('What the vulgar call
identity notoriously does not always turn out to be so. . .' 1974 p. 200).
'Kinship' is defined by the formula which Davidson offers as a criterion
of identity of events.

As kinship is an equivalence relation one would expect Taylor to shift
to identifying events *as* equivalence classes of his n-tuples under this
relation. This would have two advantages. First it would preserve the
way in which the analysis embodies Thesis (1). Second, if Davidson's
criterion really does express the principle according to which we make
our substitutions *salve veritate* of event descriptions, it would display this
additional mastery of event descriptions by making the referents of two
intersubstitutable descriptions the same. Taylor does not take this
course, but as he does not explain how this account of the principle, by

which the vulgar make their substitutions, falls short of identity, it is hard to see why the kinship relation should not be regarded as identity. In any case, Taylor's response falls with Davidson's criterion.

A second response open to this approach is more drastic in that it leads to abandoning the spirit of the analysis altogether. But it will be instructive to consider it. Not all occasions on which I play a club do I trump my partner's trick, but no one murders a man without killing him. There is a parallel here to the fact that not all doctors are football fans, but all doctors are persons. The latter case can be expressed in terms of Strawson's distinction between sortal and characterizing universals (general terms): 'doctor' can be analysed into a conjunction of a characterizing term, 'practices medicine' and a more general sortal, 'person'. This is because the principles for 'distinguishing, enumerating and reidentifying' doctors are those for persons. We might try to capitalize on the parallel.

We would not use both 'kill' and 'murder' to create an n-tuple, instead we would use only 'kill' and the appropriate characterization ('with knowledge and intention') of ' $<$ kill, Brutus, Caesar, $t_i >$ ' to represent the murder of Caesar by Brutus. A murder is evidently a characterized killing. This strategy would dictate forming an n-tuple with neither 'play a club' nor 'trump partner's trick'; 'play a card' can be characterized in different ways to produce both of these descriptions.

The problem is to determine which general terms to allow to form event sets. 'Man' can be further analysed (according to tradition) into 'rational' and 'animal'; 'animal' perhaps into 'living organism' and 'does not photosynthesize' (and/or 'is capable of locomotion'). The aim would be to arrive at a most general term—perhaps 'living organism' is one—which applies to a widest class of objects all with the same criterion of identity. Dummett (1973, pp. 75-6) calls one of these most-general general terms a 'categorical predicate'. The problem for this response on behalf of the Martin-Taylor analysis is to determine categorical predicates for events, but the choice of such predicates clearly depends on recognizing that the use of some general terms (i.e. verbs) involves the mastery of a criterion of identity (for events). The ordered-set analysis now, however, has lost its point; it no longer offers an account of event identity, but presupposes one.

Section 4

To evaluate the prospects for attacking Strawson's position along the two lines opened in Section 2 requires beginning with and attempting to elaborate the model of a feature placing language.

The remainder of this monograph will be taken up with an examination of Thesis (1) and with the attacks on it sketched earlier. Proper formulation and evaluation of the attacks requires a lengthy and complex development of model languages and artificial language users. First, something will be said about the motivation for the approach to be taken and about the path the argument will follow.

We have seen in Section 3 that if the phenomenon of an event appearing under more than one description is to be taken seriously, we must reject Thesis (2). There is more to the grasp of the identity of at least some attributive particulars than is required simply for the grasp of the semantic elements of the underlying sentences. The first thesis does not suffer directly from taking this phenomenon seriously, but the observation that more may be involved in the grasp of the identity of the further particular than in the list of semantic elements *so far given* for the underlying sentence, raises the possibility that a Martin-Taylor analysis uses an incomplete list of those elements.

This is, indeed, what Davidson has been urging, but his reasons for doing so were based on his holist approach to language. He would claim the list of elements for an underlying sentence to be incomplete because of the presence in the language of other (in particular, adverbially modified) sentences. However, once we raise questions about whether one portion of a language can be mastered without a mastery of another portion, the holist standpoint has to be dropped, especially if we are examining a thesis that the mastery of the further portion is in some way dependent on the mastery of the first portion.

To argue that the list of semantic elements of the underlying sentence is incomplete and do so in a way which undermines Thesis (1), we have to follow the direction Moravcsik indicated (p. 14, above) and argue that the mastery of the general terms of at least some underlying sentences involves more than mastery of the terms' application as represented by their extensions (either in this world or in all possible worlds.) We have already seen that Moravcsik suggests that to apply general terms such as 'is born' and 'eats' requires the ability to distinguish and count births and devourings.

When Strawson classified verbs as characterizing general terms, he had good reason. Verbs do supply principles for collecting antecedently individuated particulars. A grasp of the sentence 'Carr caught Compton out' rests on an ability to individuate men, and equips one to group together those men who have caught Compton out and those men whom Carr has caught out. But Strawson nowhere mentions that verbs appear to *supply* principles for distinguishing and counting particulars of a different kind: the grasp of 'travelled to London' may require an antecedent grasp of principles for individuating travellers, but does it not also involve a grasp of principles for 'distinguishing and counting' trips to London? Does not 'The sun rose at 6.45 a.m.' require mastery of principles for distinguishing and counting sunrises, 'John has been promoted to private first class', a mastery of principles for distinguishing and counting promotions in a soldiers's career? Cannot one count the times Carr caught Compton out, the runs Compton made before his dismissal, the bounces of a ball before it is caught? Do not such verb phrases as 'catch a ball', etc. function as sortal general terms for events?[11]

A possible response to this attack on Thesis (1) is simply to reject the idea that the ability to distinguish and count the likes of trips, sunrises, promotions, catches, runs, bounces, etc. forms an essential part of the mastery of the corresponding general terms. Burge (1972, p. 271) offers as a *sufficient condition* of a word's being a general term, 'that it be truly applicable to (or true of) each of a plural number of objects'. One might go beyond Burge here and insist that any mastery associated with a word or phrase beyond the grasp of its correct application to each of a plural number of objects does not contribute to its function as a general term. But, to succeed, the reply must establish that there are application criteria for verb phrases which can be mastered without a mastery of the identity of anything like events.

The reply acquires strength by widening the issue beyond the question whether there are separable elements in our grasp of verb phrases. Strawson argues that a corresponding separation can be made in the grasp of sortals applied to 'independent particulars'. Some events are dependent particulars for Strawson, it will be recalled, because they cannot be 'introduced into discourse' without discourse already possessing sortal terms applicable to material bodies. Material bodies (or at least spatial continuants) are not dependent on other particulars so they are independent particulars. To argue that there is a conceivable level of linguistic competence which stands to sortals as the corresponding characterizing general terms stand to such sortals as 'trip', 'catch', 'promotion', etc. is to accept that *no* term on this level functions as a sortal or characterizing term (Cf. 1963, p. 207). On this level—which, if it existed as an independent instrument of communication, would be called a 'feature-placing language'—there are no principles of identity.

If such a level of linguistic mastery is possible, then strawson presents us with a stratification of linguistic ability at the ground floor of which there are no sortals (and, indeed, no distinction between singular and general terms); on the first level of which there are sortals 'introducing' material bodies (and possibly other things); and on the second level of which are sortals introducing events (and possibly other things). As the relationship between ground and first level reflects the relationship between first and second level, the possibility of making the first separation strengthens the case for the possibility of making the second separation.

Accordingly our second chapter begins with an examination of Strawson's notion of a feature placing language. The coherence of this notion provides support for Strawson's position vis-a-vis Thesis (1). If a separation can be made between the ability to respond to an environment populated by spatial continuants and the grasp of the identity principles for such spatial continuants—for this is what a feature placer represents—then it would be reasonable to expect a similar separation between the ability to respond to an environment in which continuants change and the grasp of principles of identity for such events.

Of course the complete case for Strawson's position requires in addition a description of a model language user who represents the separation of the first and second levels, who is more sophisticated than a feature placer in that he has a grasp of principles of identity for spatial continuants and responds to changes in such things, but who does not have a grasp of principles of identity for changes or any other class of dependent particulars. What has already been done along the lines pursued on pp. 12-14—'thinking away' the use of adverbial and adjunct modification from the linguistic practice of an ordinary speaker of English—is enough to put up a strong defence of Strawson's position against a direct attack such as (b) on p. 14. But it is not a defence which does much to illuminate what a grasp of principles of identity consists in. By approaching this middle level from below, by asking what more a feature placer must be able to do if he is to be regarded as having a grasp of principles of identity for independent particulars of some kind, we stand to gain some insight into how Strawson's stratified representation is to be made out in detail as well as a more precise account of how dependent particulars depend.

Section 6 pursues a hint left by Strawson that principles of identity involve a grasp of limits and extent; it does this by applying the Calculus of Individuals to represent what must be minimally involved in such a grasp. The principle of identity for Individuals in the Calculus suggests a possible principle of reidentification, but Section 7 shows that before any such principle of identity can be used, attention must be paid to the grasp of temporal concepts, particularly to the ability to distinguish encounters with what is to be reidentified. Attempts to follow further suggestions made by Strawson require the elaboration of the Calculus itself; adding topological concepts to the theory (Section 8) provides a more adequate representation of the grasp of limits and extent and this leads to a treatment of principles of distinctness (Section 9) which is applicable to both spatial and temporal dimensions. Further elaboration (Section 10) eventually leads to a position where the model language user is able sufficiently to distinguish encounters to be able to apply a principle of reidentification.

One outcome of building the feature placer up to a level where he can apply principles of reidentification is a model which represents the separation between Strawson's two levels (Section 11). This does more than establish the conclusion tentatively drawn from the model used in this chapter; it helps to clarify issues so that attack (a) on p. 14 can be pursued. The model drawn by abstracting from the linguistic practice of an ordinary speaker of English does not show that what is left, after the abstraction, contains all that is required of an instrument of communication. Strawson laid great stress on the need for particulars which constituted a 'common and continuously extendable framework of reference', and it is far from obvious that what is left when Strawson's dependent particulars are removed is enough to constitute such a framework. The model developed in Chapter 2 can be used to begin to clarify what is required of such a framework by allowing us to ask whether the model language user could be said to possess a grasp of the identity of basic particulars.

The emphasis from this point on must be on communication, for basic particulars are required for one aspect of communication, identifying reference. But a spatio-temporal framework can be used in other enterprises. One such, which needs to be isolated and set to one side, is the use of a framework for finding one's ways about from place to place (Section 12).

The issue then becomes whether the members of an immobile community (whose members neither move nor conceive of their own mobility) could operate with Strawson's 'common and continuously extendable framework of reference' without making use of principles of identity for such things as processes, changes, states or conditions (all of which Strawson claims are not required). To show that they could not, it will be argued that although they could take what Strawson called a 'decisive conceptual step' (1963, p. 207), they cannot use the distinction they attain in taking this step to anything like the extent to which we use it (Section 15). The requirement that the distinction would have to be used as widely as we use it is a legitimate application of Strawson's own approach to basic particulars; for if the argument is not governed in this way by the attempt to see what is needed to approximate our own practice, there is no need for a framework of reference which is unified spatially as well as temporally (Section 13).

2

A Feature Placer on his Own

Section 5

The first lesson to be learned from the model of a feature placer is the importance of principles for applying more than one word to a single thing.

The first task of this chapter is to reach an understanding as to what is meant by a 'feature-placing language'. For example, the 'placing' in 'feature-placing' must not be taken literally. Strawson rules out sentences with the force of 'It rained in New York, yesterday' (placing the 'rain feature' in a place at a time) for the point of a feature placing sentence is that it avoids predicating of an identifiable subject and this sentence could be construed as predicating rain of an identifiable place-time. Strawson argues that a sentence with the force of 'It is raining here and now' can avoid having its structure construed as predication of an identifiable subject because the demonstratives 'here' and 'now' do not 'definitely identify a term'—' "Now" and "here" by themselves, set no boundaries at all. . .' (1963, p. 222). (The suggestion that identification involves a grasp of boundaries will be examined below.)

It is not, however, clear what it is for a sentence in a feature placing language 'to have the force of' a sentence in English. It would seem reasonable to require a speaker who can utter a sentence with the force of 'It is raining here and now' to be able to utter a sentence with the force of 'It is raining somewhere else' (or 'at another time'). This would seem to require a grasp of at least vague boundaries between what is 'here' and 'now' and what is not. To square this objection with Strawson's words, we will have to take the *force* of 'here' and 'now' to be simply that the speaker utters the appropriate sign for a feature when and where he encounters that feature without using a contrast between here/now and elsewhere/at another time.

To explain what he means by a 'feature' Strawson makes important use of our intuitions about mass words. Indeed, physical stuffs such as coal, snow and water are offered as paradigm examples of features. We are then invited to imagine that a non-mass word such as 'cat' might, if stripped of certain elements of its mastery, function as a feature word. The element we must imagine to be removed is the mastery of the distinction between encountering *another cat* and encountering *the same cat again*. Without this distinction it is supposed that 'cat' would function as 'snow' and 'coal' function.

This account, however, can be seen (Cartwright, 1965) to rest on an inadequate appreciation of what is involved in the grasp of words for physical stuffs. The distinction between 'the same coal' and 'more coal' requires a mastery of a principle of identity comparable to that required for the 'same cat/another cat' distinction.

Overlooking this point hinders the approach Strawson took to the conception of a feature-placing language, but the point need not be taken to undermine that conception. It is easy enough, on the one hand, to find candidates for feature concepts which do not in our adult linguistic practice involve a grasp of the 'same/more' distinction. We can, for example, imagine a feature placer responding to the appropriate stimuli with 'warm', 'cold', 'wet', 'dry', 'dark', 'light', 'hungry', etc. On the other hand, it would seem perfectly possible for a person to respond in this manner to the presence of coal, snow, water, etc., that is by producing a sign for, say, coal, when and only when he encounters coal, without a grasp of the distinction between 'same coal' and 'more coal'.

We face, however, the objection that he will not have *our* concept of coal, and not merely because the 'same/more' distinction is part of our concept. If he is not able to distinguish *the same coal* from *more coal,* it will be hard to make sense of his supposed knowledge that he faces coal. We distinguish between *coal* and *what looks like coal* by means of our knowledge of how coal behaves under various transformations, e.g. How does it feel when you handle it? How does it look when you break a piece open? Will it burn? It would seem that to possess a grasp of such transformations a person requires a grasp of the notion of 'same coal' and the contrast to 'more coal' (and 'less coal').

One may steadfastly refuse to entertain questions about how the feature placer knows he confronts coal. We can, after all, imagine a creature who is able to say 'coal' when and only when in the presence of coal. We do not have to claim he has *our* concept of coal, but since he can do *part* of what we are able to do with our concept we can say that a *correlate* of our word exists in his language. The question remains, however, whether imagining such a thing will serve a useful purpose. We can likewise imagine a feature placer responding to duplicity, courtesy, or ingenuity without a grasp of the identity of people, but including correlates of these notions in a feature placing language will do nothing to represent the grasp we have of these notions.

If there is to be a correlate of our notion of coal in the feature placing language it will have to be one whose mastery consists in being able to respond to what we take to be the immediate indicators of the presence of coal, its appearance, its smell or taste, etc. We can say the feature placer's abilities are close to ours because we can think of him as prone to be taken in by the same cleverly constructed imitations which take us in. The difference will be that when the fraud is exposed he will simply stop reporting 'coal'; we, however, will be able to judge that what we thought was coal was, after all, not coal.

It is in this spirit that we shall have to approach Strawson's invitation to consider a correlate of 'cat' in the feature-placing language (1963, p. 211). The feature placer must, first of all, lack a grasp of the distinction which corresponds to 'more coal/same coal', namely 'another cat/same cat'. Furthermore, he will be unable to discriminate between real cats and realistically stuffed or painted cats, for to recognize that a thing lives, one must recognize that it changes and to do this one must be able to distinguish between the same thing and another thing. In the case of 'cat' there is yet a further consideration: to recognize that he is in the presence of at least one cat, or cat-shaped object, must not the feature placer have some grasp of the principle of what makes one cat-shaped object distinct from another?

The strength of this point forces Strawson to admit,

> . . . not that the required type of general concept of cat is impossible, but rather that the concept must already include in itself the *basis* for the criteria of *distinctness* which we apply to particular cats. Roughly, the idea of the cat-feature, unlike that of snow, must include the idea of a characteristic shape, a characteristic pattern for the occupation of space.
>
> (1963, p. 213)

It is clear, on the one hand, that Strawson regards the feature placer as responding not to cats as such but to cat-shapes, but it is not altogether clear, on the other hand, how the basis for a distinction can be present without the distinction being mastered. However, before we can explore the hint contained in the expression 'characteristic shape, a characteristic pattern for the occupation of space', we must ask whether it is possible to respond to at least one cat-shape without a mastery of the distinction.

Consider: confronted with a pile of rope(s) we are often unable to say whether we confront one rope or many ropes. Is it not possible also to imagine a person able to respond with the word 'rope' to rope(s) (piled, coiled, scattered about) without a grasp of the principle that continuity of length makes *one* rope? Loose ends might be plainly visible; a number of short ropes might lie isolated from each other. There is no need to hold that this *must* figure in the ability of someone to report 'rope' when he encounters rope(s). Similarly, confronted with a can of worm(s) or sack of cat(s), we might be doubtful as to whether the can or sack contained one or many beasts. May we not allow a feature placer the ability to respond correctly to the presence of one or more worms or cats (worm or cat-shaped objects) without a grasp of the principle by which we distinguish one worm or cat-shaped object from another?[1]

The argument of the previous paragraph seems to succeed because 'rope' behaves both as a mass and a non-mass word. What is crucial is that if there is any rope (mass) present then regardless of how many ends are hidden or visible there will be at least one rope (non-mass) present. In a heap of worm(s) or cat(s) no single whole worm or cat may be visible and there is nothing in this situation which the feature placer could use to distinguish from the situation where no single whole worm or cat is present. The problem may be simplified by asking how the feature placer is to respond when he confronts a worm or cat, part of which is obscured by something else.

There seem to be two ways to deal with this. One is to observe that parts of cats, (heads, bodies, legs, tails) are characteristically feline and to credit the feature placer with the ability to respond to this feline characteristic. In this case he will report 'cat' when confronted with what is recognizable as a cat part regardless of whether the rest of the cat is present. *Our* ability to respond to parts of cats as such is, however, based on our grasp that the pattern which characterizes, say, a cat's head, is part of a pattern which characterizes a whole cat. What is the basic element in our grasp is better represented in a second approach to the idea of a cat-feature, viz. to say that a feature placer responds with 'cat' only to the appearance of a complete cat. There can be latitude in what is to count as a complete cat: evidently a cat's tail will not count, but a tailless cat (or a cat whose tail is not in evidence) may count as a cat. This second approach evidently fits Strawson's idea of a cat-feature, and is the approach which will be followed here.

To this general outline of a feature placer's abilities it may be objected that it is a very inadequate model of what it takes to speak a language. Far from presenting a model of a language user, what has here been described is nothing more than a complex and mysterious detection machine, a machine which can be programmed to detect and report an indefinitely extendable list of environmental features—in the way a Geiger counter detects and reports the presence of radiation. It was, however, not the aim of the model to present a complete picture of human language mastery; the aim, rather, was to isolate one very fundamental ability which is obviously involved in speaking a language. Of course the danger of this model is that one will imagine that because it isolates this ability, it also establishes a temporal priority. It is far more likely that no person's linguistic mastery ever consists entirely in abilities of this kind, not even a child's mastery at the first stage of learning to speak.[2] This will become apparent as we proceed to exploit the model to bring certain features of our own linguistic abilities into sharp relief.

It may be tempting to describe the linguistic mastery of a feature placer as consisting solely in a grasp of principles or criteria of application. To do so invites the cogent objection that it is not in order to describe the feature placer as *applying* words or signs *to anything,* as he is not equipped with a grasp of what it is to apply more than one word to the same thing. It is a symptom of this inability that, as so far described, the feature placer is unable even to form complex expressions out of simple ones; all the expressions at his command are isolated from one another. But it is possible to equip him with the alibity to form complex expressions without meeting this objection. We can equip him to form complex expressions by means of propositional connectives, conjunction, disjunction and negation. He can display his new mastery by the syntactical complexity of his utterances and by his ability to respond to questions, 'water?', 'no'; 'water or sand?', 'yes'; 'water and sand?', 'no'.[3]

But this does not equip the feature placer to apply more than one word to a single something. A grasp of when it is appropriate to utter 'cold', 'hard', 'red', and 'ball' may be extended to a grasp of a complex which is appropriate only when all four are appropriate or to the grasp of a complex which is appropriate when at least one is appropriate. But neither of these amounts to a grasp of when it is appropriate to apply all four *to one thing*. It would be appropriate, after all, to utter a conjunction of all four when, holding a rubber ball in the right hand, a piece of teak in the left, the feature placer stands in a cold puddle and has a red light shone in his eye.

One might suppose that although these four words do not in the mouth of a feature placer necessarily apply to a single spatial thing (a cold, hard, red ball), they do nevertheless apply to the same time. This however, misses the force of the objection. The feature placer lacks a grasp of the distinction between 'something is both red and hard' and 'Something is red and something is hard'. That he is able to form a conjunction when he encounters red and hard at the same time does not mean he is equipped with the distinction between 'Some time is both red and hard' and 'Some time is red and some time is hard'. It is precisely this distinction which is required if there is to be content to saying he applies more than one word to a single thing.

Evidently a grasp of what it is to apply two words to a single thing is required if the feature placer's syntax is to display even the most elementary quantificational structure, e.g. '(x)(Fx & Gx)'. In fact a feature-placing language admits of no existential generalization, for were one to suggest that the use of feature concepts, 'F', 'G' and 'H' was in fact equivalent to the use of existential statements, the suggestion could be repudiated. The use of the existential forms requires a grasp of questions of the form 'Is x (that is F) identical to or distinct from y (that is G)?' Moreover, since a singular sentence, 'Fa', entails a quantified sentence of the form '(x)(x = a & Fx)' there will be (as intended) no singular sentences in a feature-placing language. (Even in a language without existential quantifiers the use of a singular sentence requires the ability to apply both a name and a general term to a single thing.)

Singular sentences, of course, include those with more than one singular term, so the feature placer will not be able to cope with relations. We could credit a feature placer with a grasp of what might be called 'relation features'; for example he might use the word 'beach' for an expanse of water adjacent to an area of sand. But we could not assume he had a grasp of the way his report of (a) beach was related to his reports of sand and water. Lacking an ability to make relational judgements, a feature placer lacks a grasp of part and whole. Thus he could not grasp the way in which a characteristic pattern (cat-feature) contains a characteristic sub-pattern (cat-face-feature). Even if he used the English sounds 'cat' and 'cat-face' they would be as unrelated as are our words 'rat' and 'Socrates'.

A feature placer would also have very limited resources for reporting change. He could learn to use a sign whenever red gave way to blue in his visual field, but could not be credited with a grasp of what it is for a thing which is red to become blue. Nor is change of place within his grasp. To report a change of place he must be able to say of a thing, say, a man, both that it is a man and that it was in place p and is now in place p'. Without a grasp of change of place, a feature placer will be unable to discriminate between those of his successive perceptions which are the result of changes in his environment and those which are the result of changes in his own location.

Part of the motivation for investigating the notion of a feature-placing language was that it formed the ground level of Strawson's three (possibly more) level stratification of linguistic abilities. The suggestion that the ability to report events ('Carr caught the ball') might be separated from a grasp of the identity of events (Carr's catch) has now been applied to the reports of the presence of such things as coal and cats. The result of removing anything that might be put down to an understanding of an identity principle is indeed devastating, but there clearly is something which a creature who lacks all such abilities can do: he can make regulated responses to his environment, however unstructured the totality of his responses may be.

It thus appears possible to make the separation between the ground level and the superstructure of what in Strawson's theoretical representation is the edifice of linguistic mastery. This makes clear the sort of separation Strawson proposed between the first and second levels and makes that separation seem more plausible. A description of a further model language user who operates on the first level (above ground) without operating on the second would represent the separation of those two levels. But it was argued above that to constitute a complete defence of Strawson's position such a model language user would need principles of identity which give him access to the grasp of a unified spatio-temporal framework within which he is able to relate the reports of other creatures of similar linguistic abilities. So far our first model language user, the feature placer, has tended to highlight only what it is to be completely without identity principles.

This does not mean that we are still completely in the dark about what it is to be in possession of identity principles. In amplifying Strawson's position on events (above, pp. 12‒14) it was suggested that the grasp of the identity of events will be manifested in the use of predicate modifiers. The suggestion drew upon an article (1971, pp. 65‒74) where Strawson argued that the existence of principles for collecting particulars under general terms was sufficient for treating quantification over those particulars seriously. The investigation of the notion of a feature placing language has reinforced this suggestion, but has also revealed that its development involved some misplaced emphasis. Without criteria of identity the feature placer is unable to apply more than one word to a single thing. His limitations are a generalization of what it was claimed were the limitations of a person who lacks a grasp of event identity, (above, pp. 25f.) But it is now clear that as well as emphasizing principles which collect particulars (Strawson's example': 'qualities desirable in a date') equal emphasis will have to be given to the importance of principles by which more than one word or phrase may be applied to one thing.[4]

Section 6
Mereology provides a basis for representing a minimal grasp of limits and extent.

The next stage in this investigation involves seeing how we might elaborate the model of a feature placer so that he will reflect a grasp of the identity of something, i.e. so that he will possess at least the ability to apply more than one word to a single thing. Strawson (1963, pp. 224 ff.) examines a 'surrogate' for the conceptual apparatus we actually use, a surrogate which seems to provide a simplified model of what we are after. This is the suggestion that we add to the abilities of a feature placer a grasp of the identity of places and times, so that our model language user is able to apply more than one word to a single place or time. He would, thus, be able literally to *place* features in spatial and temporal regions and the syntax of his simple utterances will have to reflect this ability by an increase in complexity to something of the form, 'It ϕ s, p, t'—a sentence form locating feature, ϕ, in place, p, during time, t.

When we turn to consider the details of what a grasp of the identity of places and times consists in we find ourselves constrained by the abstract nature of places and times. Because there are no answers to such bare questions as 'What are the limits of a volume of space or period of time?'

> . . . we must have recourse to the features which occupy or occur in space and time, to give us our limits and our persistences.
>
> (1963, p. 224)

that is, we take feature placers,

> . . . as it were, to borrow criteria of *distinctness* for places from the feature-concepts. . .
>
> (*ibid.* p. 226)

To follow this suggestion we must seek answers to three questions—questions which, unfortunately, Strawson does not explicitly raise or try to answer.
(1) Can we assume that 'places' and 'times' will be structured as our own spatio-temporal concepts and is this structure something else which is 'borrowed' from feature concepts?
(2) If 'places' and 'times' depend for their distinctness on features, what gives us the right to speak of 'places' and 'times' over and above features?
(3) What must a feature placer be able to do to display his mastery of the

notions of 'place' and 'time' in addition to his ability to report the presence of features?

There is ample basis on which to infer how Strawson would approach question (3). The reason we must turn to features to find the principles which distinguish one 'place' or 'time' from another is that otherwise we have no answers to questions about limits and persistences (extent). This much is clear, but can more be said about what the grasp of limits and extent consists in?

In this section I will offer what I will call a 'minimal' account. More may be said about what is involved in the ability to deal with limits and extent and in Section 8 I will try to spell out that 'more'. Here I wish to consider only a necessary part of what it is to be able to deal with limits and extent. To make a mistake about the extent of something is either to treat it as including something it does not include or to overlook something which it does include. A creature which cannot relate part and whole cannot be said to have a grasp of limits and extent. In offering this much answer to question (3), I will introduce the model of a feature placer (hereafter, a 'feature *P*lacer') who has graduated to a grasp of something which I will call '*P*lace' and '*T*ime' to distinguish from our concepts of place and time.

If a feature Placer is to display a grasp of the limits and extent of Places and Times, he must be able to give reports of the part/whole structure of such things. If it takes a feature to distinguish a Place or Time, it will take a different feature to distinguish a part of that Place or Time. Thus a feature Placer must be able to report certain relations between features, but clearly he must be able to do a good deal more. He must be able to report when two features determine the *same* Place (Time), and more: he must be able to report when, say, the Places determined by features ϕ, ψ, and χ together exhaust the Places determined by feature π.

This last requirement gives us a clear two-part answer to question (2). Places and Times may be distinguished from features first of all because more than one feature may determine the same Place or Time. Secondly, if a feature Placer is to be able to make a report of the form illustrated at the end of the previous paragraph, he will have to recognize that a Place (Time) may be determined by a 'sum' of several Places (Times). That is to say, Places (Times) are not only determined by individual features, but may also be determined indirectly by a 'sum' of Places (Times). In these two respects, at least, we are justified in speaking of Places and Times over and above features although, ultimately, all Places and Times depend for their distinctness on features.

The 'minimal' ability to determine limits and extent of Places and

Times consists, therefore, in this: the ability to make judgements in which spatial and temporal regions, determined by the presence or absence of features, are related as parts and wholes. What it is for the objects of some range to be related as parts and wholes can be given a formal characterization by drawing on a branch of logic known as mereology. Before the end of this section one development of mereology will be outlined so that we will have a firmer hold on precisely what the creature, to be called here a 'feature Placer' can do. But several other matters need to be considered first.

We can now answer question (1) by observing that our own spatial and temporal concepts have a part-whole structure, so that the feature Placer's concepts share this much structure with our own. On the other hand, the complexity of our spatio-temporal concepts evidently extends well beyond part-whole structure to include, for example, the topological relations which are treated in Section 8 below, as well as the structure of three dimensional affine or Euclidean geometry, which will play no role in the development of this monograph. In saying the feature Placer's spatio-temporal concepts share with our own a part-whole structure we must be careful not to assume implicitly that they share any more than this, unless and until more is added in further developments.

Question (1) also asked whether the structure attributed to the Places and Times of the feature Placer is something which is 'borrowed' from the feature concepts. The answer to this is clearly 'no'. The feature Placer is required to recognize certain relations holding between features and to co-ordinate reports based on that recognition to an extent which is completely beyond the feature placer. Neither of these abilities can be simply borrowed from the ability to respond correctly to the presence of a feature; both represent entirely new elements of linguistic mastery. The feature Placer borrows from the abilities of the feature placer only to the extent that his performance clearly presupposes doing what the feature placer can do.

The feature Placer is more than a versatile detection machine for he somehow manages to report the spatial and temporal coincidences of what he detects. If he uses different sense organs to do this, we will have to credit him with the ability to co-ordinate these into a single perceptual field, rather as though tactile information could be fed into our visual fields and we could 'see' that wherever it was ginger red (or cats) it was warm, soft and dry, without taking any account of running our hands over anything to acquire this information. This is not completely far-fetched; after all, we take no account of the minute scanning movements of our eyeballs. The co-ordination of a creature's sense organs might exist on a similarly automatic and subconscious level.

The feature Placer's ability to report relations between Times also requires some comment. Judgements about the relations between Places must be based on relations which appear within a feature Placer's perceptual field at given time, i.e. synchronous relations. The ability to respond to what is in his perceptual field at a given moment, even to relations in that field, will by itself provide the feature Placer with no basis for recognizing temporal relations of part and whole.[5] For this the feature Placer will have somehow to retain and be able to recall what has been present in his field, so that he can survey this in a single span of 'memory' and on this basis report whether, for example, the Time distinguished by light (light feature) is part of the Time distinguished by warm (warmth feature). This need not be 'memory' in anything like our sense of the word. What is surveyed in this 'span' is not temporally ordered. Just as Euclidean geometry involves structure which is not included in that treated by mereology and is, hence, beyond the feature Placer, so temporal ordering involves structure which is not captured by mereology and no grasp which involves such ordering can, as yet, be imputed to the feature Placer. If he experienced warmth without light, he has been given no basis for judging that this came before or after his experience of warmth with light, and he will be provided with nothing of the sort until section 10.

There is no point in trying to elaborate on the mechanisms which enable a feature Placer to make the reports he does. What is required is an account of his abilities in terms of verbal display. To display his grasp of Places and Times a feature Placer will require a sufficiently complex syntax. To be sure, a large variety of syntactical structure would serve here, but I will deal with only one rather artificial example which draws on a formal development of mereology. As mereology will prove a framework for subsequent developments in the feature Placer's abilities, it will be useful to set out briefly the history and motivation of this branch of formal logic.

The subset relation of set theory expresses what it is for one set to be *part of* another. This relation is definable from the primitive membership relation ε:

$$A \subseteq B =_{df.} (x)(x \; \varepsilon \; A \to x\varepsilon \; B).$$

But there is no reason from a formal point of view why ' $\subseteq$ ' has to be defined rather than primitive. One could use some of the theorems, in which ' $\subseteq$ ' appears, as axioms, and set out to treat 'sets' as objects which are related by ' $\subseteq$ ', as well as by intersection and union (which are definable from ' $\subseteq$ '). The result would not be the same as if one had begun with the 'ε' relation; one cannot define a relation with the properties of ε in such a theory. Although it might help one's intuition to regard the objects of the theory as sets of something (e.g. points), they would not be sets *of anything* from the point of view of the theory. This would, in fact, be the interest of the theory as a formal theory of parts: in order to regard a leg as part of a table, we do not think of either as a set of anything. If one had a formal theory of classes which did not treat them as composed of members, but which captured the union and part (sub-set) structure, one could apply this theory to ordinary things and use the abstract structure it described to elucidate the required notion of 'part' and 'sum'.

Because the theory is to be developed without the membership relation holding between individuals of the theory, the theory will not involve relations between objects which differ in (simple) type in the sense of Russell's theory of types. Since Russell called the objects of lowest type, 'individuals', when Leonard and Goodman published the sort of theory here envisioned, they called it the 'Calculus of Individuals'.[7]

Knowing the historical background to the use of the word 'individual' may make it easier to accept that under certain interpretations of the theory some unlikely individuals appear. If a pen and a garden gate are 'individuals' of the (interpreted) theory, then so is their fusion, a single physically disconnected individual. Leonard and Goodman described their concepts of 'individual' and 'class' as 'different devices for distinguishing one segment of the total universe from all that remains' (p. 45), and this can be accepted as a explanation of a technical idea without prejudice to the question of what we might ordinarily mean by 'an individual'. (To warn that the word 'individual' has been borrowed for technical purposes, the initial letter will be capitalized.)

The basics of the Calculus of Individuals (*CI,* for short) are very easy to set down. There are three interdefinable relations any one of which may be taken as primitive and the axioms and definitions adjusted accordingly: '$x \subseteq y$' ('x is a part of y') will be taken as primitive. The first axiom connects the primitive relation to identity,

$$\text{Ax} \quad 1 \quad (x)(y)(x \subseteq y \ \& \ y \subseteq x \rightarrow x = y)$$

Then two defined relations are added,

$$\text{Df} \quad 1 \quad x \ o \ y =_{df.} (\exists z)(z \subseteq x \ \& \ z \subseteq y) \qquad (\text{'}x \text{ overlaps } y)$$
$$\text{Df} \quad 2 \quad x \ Z \ y =_{df.} \sim(x \ o \ y) \qquad (\text{'}x \text{ is discrete from } y\text{'})$$

The next axiom connects the primitive to the first defined relation,

$$\text{Ax} \quad 2 \quad (x)(y)(x \subseteq y \leftrightarrow (z)(z \ o \ x \rightarrow z \ o \ y).$$

The final axiom requires the definition of the 'fusion' of class α, of Individuals,

$$\text{Df} \quad 3 \quad x \, \text{Fu}\alpha = {}_{\text{df.}} (z)(z \, \mathbf{Z} \, x \rightarrow (y)(y \, \varepsilon \, \alpha \rightarrow z \, \mathbf{Z} \, y));$$

the axiom then guarantees the existence of the fusion for any non-empty class α,

$$\text{Ax} \quad 3 \quad (\exists x)(x \, \varepsilon \, \alpha) \rightarrow (\exists y)(y \, \text{Fu}\alpha).$$

Fusion is meant to function like class union; to have something which behaves like class intersection one defines the 'nucleus' of a class, α, (all of whose members have a common part),

$$\text{Df} \quad 4 \quad x \, \text{Nu}\alpha = {}_{\text{df.}} (z)(z \, \varepsilon \, x \rightarrow (y)(y \, \varepsilon \, \alpha \rightarrow z \subseteq y)).$$

The nucleus of a class all of whose members have a common part can be shown to be the fusion of all such common parts, so Ax 3 also provides the theory with nuclei.

The concern here will not be with what theorems can be proved from these axioms, but with how the calculus may be interpreted, and there is no need to be restricted by any particular interpretation. In the presence of Ax 2, Ax 1 is provably equivalent to

$$(x)(y)((z)(z \subseteq y \leftrightarrow z \subseteq x) \rightarrow x = y), \quad (*)$$

(which is the form of set theory's Axiom of Extensionality). We can say no more within the theory about the identity of Individuals than is expressed in Ax 1 or can be proved, like (*), from the axioms. But the theory does thereby offer an account of identity and in the sequel much will be learned from this account and from a study of its limitations.

Definitions 3 and 4 and Axiom 3 require careful comment not only because of the special impact they have on interpreting *CI,* but because they appear to conflict with the claim made above that the theory does not involve relations between objects which differ in type. All three involve a variable—conspicuously marked by a Greek letter—which ranges over *classes* of Individuals. The presence of such a variable, however, does not, strictly speaking, make the calculus a theory of type-heterogeneous objects. In the version of the calculus which appears in Goodman, 1966 Goodman turns the axiom into one giving the existence of a fusion of all Individuals satisfying any given predicate. The 'classes', in other words, can be thought of as virtual classes—$x \, \varepsilon \, \alpha$ is always eliminable in favour of Fx, because there is always a predicate such that $\alpha = \{x : Fx\}$.

Axiom 3 can thus be thought of an analogous to, say, the axiom of subsets in *ZF* set theory or the axiom of induction in first order arithmetic. That is, Axiom 3 is not *one* axiom but a schema which avoids quantification over predicates (or sets) by laying down a separate axiom for each predicate (set). First order arithmetic and *ZF* set theory can avoid second order axioms by means of such schemata and similarly *CI* can be seen to avoid becoming a theory involving objects of a higher type by analogous means. This is very important from the point of view of Goodman's programme, the aim of which was to work entirely (if possible) within a type-homogeneous framework.

The use which *CI* makes of two kinds of variables means that giving an interpretation of the theory is somewhat more involved than it would be if *CI* were a straightforward first-order theory. In addition to saying what the Individual variables are to range over and interpreting the primitive relation, one has to say something about the Greek variables as well. This can be done in a number of ways. If one is not constrained by Goodman's programme one might (depending on the domain of the interpretation) be faced with choosing whether to have fusions of all finite sets, of countably infinite sets, or of *all* sets of Individuals whatsoever. If one preferred to bypass sets and stick to predicates, one would have to have at hand some account of the language in which the predicates were expressed.

Once one has settled the range of the Greek variables and hence what fusions one will allow, all one needs in order to provide an interpretation of the calculus is a (possibly virtual) class, D, the elements of which will be called Individuals , a relation on the elements of D to interpret $\subseteq$ and enough elements in D to ensure that if α is guaranteed a fusion, then there is a representative of that fusion in D. It is instructive to compare *CI* in this respect to the closely related theory of Boolean algebras. A Boolean algebra (a model of the theory) requires a relation, $\leq$, which behaves like '$\subseteq$' and definable operators $\vee$ (join) and $\wedge$ (meet) which behave respectively like the fusion and nucleus of a two element class of Individuals. A Boolean algebra, however, must also have a null-element, O, with the property $(x)(O \leq x)$ and also a unit, 1, with the property $(x)(x \leq 1)$ and each element x must have a complement $-x$ such that $x \wedge -x = 0$ and $x \vee -x = 1$.

Apart from an Individual which functions like O, all this is available to *CI* providing there are sufficient classes over which fusions exist. This is because the unit of *CI* (i.e. an Individual of which every Individual is a part) can be taken as the fusion of the class of all Individuals, and the complement of x as the fusion of the class $\{y: y \mathbin{\mathsf{Z}} x\}$. In the case where *CI* can form fusions of only finite classes, however, a model of *CI* will not necessarily have a unit if the class of Individuals is infinite, and nothing ensures every Individual will have a complement in that case. A

Boolean algebra with only finite meets and joins must still be equipped with a unit and complements.

It is common practice to be as generous as possible with the range of the Greek variables so that the fusion of any class whatever is available. In this case any model of *CI* differs from a (complete) Boolean algebra only in lacking the null-element. This lack is the result of allowing nuclei to be formed only for classes whose members all contain a common part. Not having a null-element makes for a less appealing mathematical structure (e.g. the operation of forming nuclei is not everywhere defined), but this does not matter for present purposes.

An obviously relevant interpretation of *CI*, because it shows how *CI* may be used to capture the structure of our spatial concepts, is one taking the domain of Individuals as ordinary physical objects, together with Individuals representing the fusions of arbitrary classes of physical objects, and interpreting the relation $\subseteq$ as 'is an arbitrary and not necessarily self-connected part of'. One could also restrict $\subseteq$ to 'is an arbitrary but self-connected part of' and admit the fusions only of classes each of whose elements was connected to at least one other element of the class. This is the flexibility of *CI*. ('Physical object' and 'self-connected', like 'space-time region', are not concepts formalised in *CI*.)

We must now consider how *CI* is to be interpreted so as to reflect the abilites of a feature Placer. The places and times to which Strawson's language user is supposed to attach features when he uses sentences of the form 'It ϕs, *p*, *t*' are supposed to have their limits and extent determined by features. Nothing in the syntactical form, 'It ϕs, *p*, *t*', reveals this dependence which places and times have on features. This can, however, be reflected in our interpretation of *CI* in terms of Times and Places, if assuming the feature Placer has a vocabulary of feature words, 'ϕ', 'ψ', 'χ', . . .; we supply him with operators on feature words, represented by *P( )* and *T( )*, which apply to feature words to produce a term designating a Place and Time respectively, e.g. 'P(ϕ)' will be read 'the Place of ϕ'. This will provide the interpretation of the Individual variables of *CI*. The Greek variables will represent lists of Places and Times. Thus all Place (and Time) designating terms will be generated either by the application of *P( )* (*T( )*) to feature words, or by the application of the operators *Fu* and *Nu* to lists consisting entirely of Place (Time) designators. The feature Placer's feature vocabulary is finite, so there will be available to him a Place, *U*, (the fusion of all Places designated by something of the form 'P(ϕ)', where 'ϕ' is a feature word) which will function as a unit for his *CI* structure of Places. A similar unit is available for the *CI* structure of Times, but only *U* will be used in subsequent developments (see Section 8).

The designating expressions of the feature Placer's language will enter two place atomic predicate expressions which we can represent by $\subseteq$, o and Z. We will carry over from the feature placer the ability to form truth functional complexes and then take it that the axioms and definitions of CI will supply the account of the formal relations between these relation-expressions and between them and identity. Because two distinct Places may be part of the same Place, or a single Place form parts of two distinct Places, a feature Placer will certainly have to be able to apply two phrases to the same thing,[8] thus the obstacle which prevented the feature placer from mastering quantifiers is not present in this case. He will, moreover, have a means of redescribing Places (and Times). A feature may distinguish the same Place (Time) as that distinguished by another feature, or by a combination of features via a fusion or nucleus. Descriptions of the same Place (Time) may be substituted one for another and the principle which governs this is contained in the axioms and theorems (e.g. (*)) of CI. Any implicit grasp of identity represented by the theory CI will in turn rest on the grasp of atomic sentences of the form $P(\phi) \subseteq P(\psi)$.

Davidson's attempt to specify a criterion of identity for events came to rest, in a similar fashion, on causal relations between events. What spoiled the attempt (pp. 6–7 above) was 'the principle of the nomological character of causality'. One could not settle the question whether a and b designated events related as cause and effect without a law relating the descriptions a and b, *or* a criterion of when a designated the same event as c and d as b and a law relating c and d. In the present context no similar difficulty presents itself. The judgement whether $P(\phi) \subseteq P(\psi)$ may be made on the basis of the direct apprehension of a relation between features ϕ and ψ.[9] However, what the feature Placer can achieve with his direct apprehension will prove to be limited in significant respects.

Section 7

The model language user of Section 6 has a principle of reidentification at his disposal, but lacks nearly everything he would need to make use of it.

Strawson, of course, did not develop the idea of borrowing criteria of distinctness for places from feature concepts in the way suggested in Section 6. He took, moreover, a very dim view of the prospects for using this idea as a foundation of an account of the principles we do use. Such principles, he emphasized, must provide for the identity of particulars through time (1963, p. 227) and he saw no resources for 'conveying' this 'idea'. The present development is clearly vulnerable to this criticism, but it is not without resources.

The vulnerability arises from the close way the identity of a Place, say $P(\phi)$, is tied to the features which distinguish its parts. If different features come to distinguish parts of $P(\phi)$, or some features cease to distinguish parts, then at this later time $P(\phi)$ cannot be the Place distinguished by ϕ at the earlier time. Faced by black cats on a white background, a feature Placer will assent to the query, '$P(\text{cats}) = P(\text{black})$?'. When a ginger cat is added to the scene he will dissent; when the ginger cat departs he assents once again.

A feature Placer is also able to retain experience in order to report on temporal relations. His reports of Place identities could also be based on retained experience. The difference this would make is that once he has encountered something like coal, regardless of whether he now confronts any such thing, he will not assent to '$P(\text{black}) \subseteq P(\text{cat})$?', and once he has encountered a ginger cat, even though the cat has departed from the scene, he no longer assents to '$P(\text{cat}) \subseteq P(\text{black})$?'. But this does not greatly alter the situation. Instead of the identity principle applying to the Places within his perceptual field *at* some one time, it now applies to accumulated experience *up to* some one time. Any immediate experience of spatial relations between features, which is inconsistent with what has hitherto accumulated, occasions a revision in his judgement of the identity of some Places.

Strawson's way of explaining the difficulty he foresaw for his approach did not amount to the difficulties set out in the previous two paragraphs. Strawson claimed that 'borrowing criteria of distinctness' would work only

> . . . so long as we are concerned with distinguishing particulars at an instant or during a period over which their position and boundaries remain unchanged.
>
> (1963, p. 227)

The notion of boundary is not adequately captured in the present minimal account of 'limit and extent' (improvements on this are to be made in the next section) and change of position is completely beyond a feature Placer. There is nothing he can do so far to display a grasp of position, either his own or that of anything in his experience. A Place is neither a position nor the occupier of a position; a distinction of this kind is simply not available.

Although a feature Placer is ill-equipped to make use of it, there is a basis for a principle of reidentification of Places: The feature ϕ distinguishes the same Place at one time as at another if and only if all parts of the Place distinguished at the first time are parts of the Place distinguished at the second time and *vice versa*. What distinguishes parts of $P(\phi)$ at the two times are, of course, features which distinguish Places overlapping $P(\phi)$, so these must be the same at both times, but this is not all. If two Places overlapping $P(\phi)$ overlap each other *and* $P(\phi)$, they determine a part of $P(\phi)$ which they would not if all three did not overlap (See Figure 1).

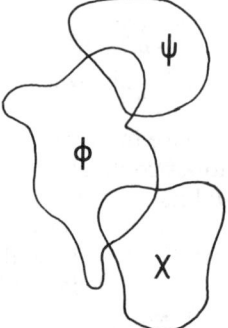 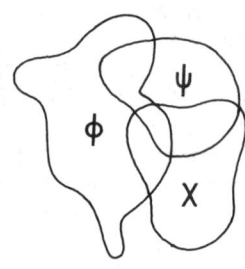

Figure 1

In the following this principle of reidentification for Places will be summed up by saying that two Places distinguished at different times are the same Place if and only if their parts are distinguished by the *same disposition of features*.

This principle of reidentification for Places is based in an obvious way on the identity principle (*) of *CI*, but it is a principle which operates outside *CI* since a theory of this kind does not have a temporal dimension. It is, after all, metatheory which compares distinct interpretations of a theory and *any* change of disposition of features changes the interpretation of *CI* which Places constitute. The proposed principle is one to be used for identifying Individuals *across* interpretations. How this principle is to function in relation to *CI* is clear enough, but objections may be raised to the whole apparatus as a model of a principle of identity.

One objection is that it is not possible to say different things about the same Place. Interpreted strictly this is not even true. The same Place, *P*(slimy) may be part of *P*(wet), discrete from *P*(dry) and overlap *P*(cold). A Place may be redescribed as a fusion of parts. It is, on the other hand, correct to say that *incompatible* things cannot be said of the same Place at different times. It is not possible to say that *P*(slimy) overlaps *P*(cold) at one time and that the *same Places* are discrete at another. (If they are discrete at a later time, the singular terms formed by *P*( ) designate different Places.) This situation will be remedied as more developments are made in the model of a feature Placer. But this is, in any case, an unreasonable demand to make on a principle of identity. It is tantamount to holding that only what Aristotle would have classified as a primary reality or substance can *have* a principle of identity.[10]

A more serious objection is that the grasp of the principle of identity for Places will play no role whatsoever in determining the correctness of making a report about Places. All sentences in a feature Placer's language are (assertion functional) complexes of atomic sentences expressing ⊆ relations between Places and these are correct in virtue of a direct apprehension of relations between features. The sentence '*P*(warm) ⊆ *P*(wet)' may constitute a correct report at different times although because of change in the disposition of features *neither* *P*(warm) nor *P*(wet) is the same Place at one time as at the other.

This objection has a sound basis, but it does not reveal a shortcoming of the proposed identity principle but rather in the ability of the feature Placer to make use of such a principle. The operator '*P*( )' produces singular terms which are ambiguous unless taken as indexicals, i.e. to designate a part of the feature Placer's perceptual field at the time of utterance. Even to begin to make use of this principle of reidentification, a feature Placer must be able to distinguish the Place determined by a feature at one time from that determined by that feature at another time. His '*P*( )' operator must be made a function of features *and* times; he requires, that is, a co-ordination between his spatial and temporal notions.

It is useless, however, to turn to the temporal notions the feature Placer already has, namely Times, and attempt to say what it would be to co-ordinate the grasp of these with the '*P*( )' operator. Times constitute a domain of objects with entirely the wrong structure to make the required distinctions between Places. To begin with, Times suffer from a shortcoming which afflicts Places. New experience is likely to upset accepted identity reports. If the feature Placer has always experienced light and warmth together (not necessarily in the same Place), then he will assent to 'T(light) = T(warmth)?'; but as soon as one appears without the other, two Times which were the same become distinct. Identity statements involving Times have to be confined to some definite span of the feature Placer's 'memory'.

When new experience is added to some span of 'memory' on which Time-identity reports have been based, a feature Placer can simply make new reports as though the old reports had not been made. This certainly does not amount to relating new experience to old, however. If a feature Placer is to cope with an expanding experience, any definite span of his memory must be structured in such a way as to leave a place for new experience. Our time is linearly ordered by the 'before' relation; any span of experience is so ordered and new experience is placed 'after' such a span. It would seem a straight-forward matter to structure a span of the feature Placer's memory in this way so as to leave a place in the structure for new experience. As it turns out, it is anything but a straightforward matter.

The parts of a span of a feature Placer's 'memory' are distinguished by features. Unless features *make* the distinction, a feature Placer is not able to divide his experience into two parts one of which came before the other. The features ϕ, ψ and χ might distinguish discrete Times within a span of 'memory' and these Times might be orderable by 'before' so that $T(\phi)$ came before $T(\psi)$ and $T(\chi)$, and $T(\psi)$ before $T(\chi)$, etc. But equally these discrete Times could be intermingled, a part of $T(\phi)$ before $T(\psi)$, then more $T(\phi)$, then a spell of $T(\chi)$, a spell of $T(\psi)$, more $T(\chi)$, more $T(\phi)$, etc. In describing this situation I have relied on an ability we have to distinguish happenings which the feature Placer completely lacks. If no distinct features distinguish these disconnected periods of ϕ, ψ and χ, they count for the feature Placer as three (and no more) Times—three Times which are not ordered by 'before'.

In our array of temporal concepts seasons are closest to Times (that is 'seasons' in the sense in which there are *only* four seasons); springtime occurs both before and after wintertime. If spring were a feature concept, a feature Placer could distinguish one spring-Time from another only if these Times were distinguished by the simultaneous occurrence of distinct features. This might, with luck, distinguish (over a two year period) this year's spring and last year's spring, but not in such a way that the two spring-Times could not appear as parts of new experience. To encounter the same combination of features is to 'return' to the same Time. (The inverted commas are necessary because there is no distinctness between what was left and that to which he 'returned'.) A feature Placer is in no position even to judge that features or feature-

Times recur or are re-encountered unless he has some basis for distinguishing the occasions on which they occur.

There is, thus, not enough distinctness between Times—they are insufficiently particular—to be structured by 'before', in order that a feature Placer could be enabled to cope with an expanding experience. In an expanding experience nothing would secure a Time in a transitive asymmetric relation structure. However fine a combination of features distinguishes a Time, that combination may be repeated and thus outflank any upper bound set on the Time. The only temporal items a feature Placer has can sprawl all over his temporal framework.

A glance back at the notion of Place will reveal that a similar problem will afflict any attempt to use Places to constitute a spatial framework extending beyond the feature Placer's immediate experience. Places will sprawl all over such a framework. They will behave like the giant scattered particulars which Quine proposed as the referents of mass terms (1960, pp. 99ff.). But they will not be particulars which 'occupy' many places; they and their parts *are* what Places there are. There is no distinction between occupier and occupied. Places have a mereological structure, but this is not all the structure required of a space. There is, it will be seen shortly, no way for a feature Placer to report even on whether a Place is sprawling and scattered or clumped together in a connected whole.

It will take the remaining three sections of this chapter to equip a feature Placer with temporal notions that will enable him to cope with an expanding experience. Without such an ability the model of a feature Placer will teach us very little more about our own use of principles of identity. In the process, improvements will be made on the account of the grasp of limits and extent which will, among other things, enable a feature Placer to report on whether a Time is scattered or has its parts connected together.

Section 8

Elementary topological notions can be added to mereology to arrive at a more adequate representation of the grasp of limits and extent.

Another look at Strawson's development of what I have called the feature-Placing Language suggests that the limitations we have encounterd over the distinctness of Places and Times (i.e. their insufficient particularity) may have arisen because we have failed to exploit all that may be borrowed from feature concepts. Strawson writes as though a feature Placer will be able to make reports which 'we should normally express by saying, "There are just three ϕs in this ψ now" ' (1960, p. 226). Setting aside difficulties which have arisen over distinguishing 'now' from other Times, the feature Placer of the previous section can make such a report, but only if there are three other features, χ_1, χ_2 and χ_3 which distinguish the ϕ-Places. Strawson, however, seems to be suggesting that the distinguishing features are unnecessary, that at least some feature-concepts will provide a basis for distinguishing instances of those concepts without the need to rely on distinguishing coincident features. Nor is there any suggestion that what the feature Placer reports amounts to another feature, e.g. 'threefold cat'. (The remarks on 'relation features', p. 34 above, will also apply to these 'perceptual numbers'.)

What Strawson seems to have the feature Placer doing here is exploiting that '*basis* for the criteria of *distinctness*', which he said was included in feature concepts which 'include the idea of a characteristic shape, a characteristic pattern for the occupation of Space', (hereafter this will be abbreviated to 'characteristic pattern'). To deal with cat-Places must not the feature Placer have the basis for isolating at least one cat from its surroundings?

Strawson does not explicity say that only a feature-concept, ϕ, which includes the characteristic pattern will provide the basis for distinguishing ϕ-Places without the help of other features, but he says enough to excuse one for thinking that this is his view. After he introduces the report, 'There are just three ϕs in the ψ now', he immediately goes on to consider this in the light of a distinction between two conventions (see footnote 8) which applies only to those feature-concepts which include the characteristic pattern. Further, no concept (e.g. snow) which does not include the characteristic pattern 'of itself provides a principle for distinguishing, enumerating and reidentifying particulars of a sort' (1963, p. 208; see also p. 213). 'Of itself' allows that 'drift' and 'expanse', etc. may combine with 'snow' to distinguish particulars.

One might object to what appears to be Strawson's view along these lines: the use of the feature-concept *snow* carries the basis of a criterion for distinguishing snow particulars which is every bit as effective as the basis which is supposed to be included in the grasp of the cat-shape feature. It happens not to be one we use, but that does not mean it is not usable. We must bear in mind that, e.g., an expanse of snow depends for its distinctness, in part, on the snow—on how far it extends. What prevents one from relying entirely on this principle to isolate one snow instance from another? The limits of each such instance will be set by where snow stops and something else begins. If a feature Placer has the ability to recognize the limits and extent of Places which are snow, he could learn to distinguish and perhaps to count, self-connected regions of snow. 'Snow' in this respect is in no way inferior to 'cat'.

Strawson might well maintain that 'self-connected region' carries the principle of distinctness, not 'snow', but this defence looks weak. It is the feature-concept itself which seems to be setting the limits of the instances of snow and doing so without relying on a characteristic pattern. A more convincing way to deploy this defence would be to point out that 'self-connected region' in fact *is* a pattern of which the feature Placer cannot as yet make use to distinguish Places or Times.

To see why it is possible to make this claim consider two pairs of snow regions, the right hand one of each pair distinguished from the left by falling in a shadow (figure 2).

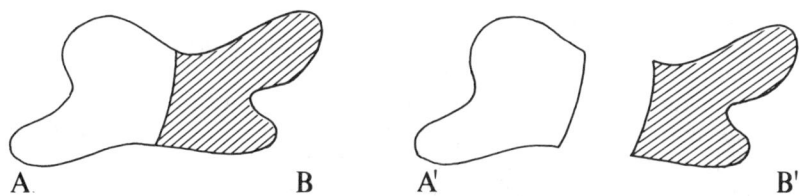

A   B   A'   B'

Figure 2

The feature Placer should count the left pair as one self-connected region of snow and the second pair as two such regions. But the feature Placer is not equipped to distinguish these two cases, each pair represents two discrete snow Places. (The same considerations apply to any attempt to use connectedness or continuity of occurrence to distinguish, say, periods of warmth or light.)

This makes plain the sense in which the feature Placer's grasp of limits and extent is 'minimal'. His grasp of what is included and what is not included in a Place or Time does not include a grasp of where a Place or Time begins and ends; that is to say, he cannot judge which things outside a Place (or Time) lie on the boundary or touch that Place (or Time) and which of the parts of the Place (or Time) lie touching the outside and which lie in the interior. If the feature Placer could recognize that the snow pair A, B lie on each other's frontier, he would be in a position to count A and B as belonging to one self-connected region.

CI provided a theoretical representation of the minimal grasp the feature Placer had of limits and extent, and there is some point in trying to provide a similar representation of the more complex grasp which would involve the notions of 'frontier' and 'connection'. On the one hand, we stand to gain insight into how instances of a feature concept such as snow may be distinguished and, on the other hand, a fully-fledged grasp of a concept involving a characteristic pattern will also involve an ability to judge where the frontier of an instance of the pattern will fall.

A place to look for material for the theoretical representation we require is point set topology where an elementary notion is the connectedness of a region of space. To apply directly concepts from this branch of mathematics would require treating Places and Times as sets of points and singling out some of these sets as *open*. (There are restrictions on what sets of open sets constitute a topological structure: finite intersections and arbitrary unions of open sets must also be open sets.) The point sets together with the designation of the open sets form a topological space. A region is connected if (treated as a sub-space) it cannot be divided exhaustively into two disjoint non-empty open sets. (See Mendelson 1962, Chapters 3 and 4.)

One virtue of CI as a theoretical representation of the minimal grasp of limits and extent is that it is plausible to use the primitive notion of the theory to represent a direct apprehension of relations between features. Thus there is an answer to the question, 'what does the feature Placer's grasp of "$P(\phi) \subseteq P(\psi)$" consist in?'. It will not be as easy to answer the question, 'what does a grasp of Places as sets of mathematical (ideal) points consist in ?'. On the other hand, Individuals in the theory CI have a structure which is close to that of set theory; this suggests that we might try adapting the concepts of elementary topology to extend the theory CI so that it acquired the relevant structure of a topological space. We could do this, perhaps, by adding a new primitive relation—one of which it would be plausible to say there could be a direct apprehension—together with axioms which characterized an implicit grasp of the relations between this new primitive notion and the rest of CI. This is what I propose to do here; as with the presentation of CI, I shall not develop the theory, merely indicate its general shape by discussing a possible list of axioms.[11]

Building on the above account of the identity and structure of Places and Times, I shall take it that a feature Placer could acquire the ability to recognize and report where or when one feature-Place or Time occurred wholly *inside* another. This relation will be represented by a new primitive symbol to be added to *CI,* written '$x \lhd y$' and read '*x* lies on the interior of *y*'. The relation is here illustrated in two dimensions by I of figure 3, but not by II or III.

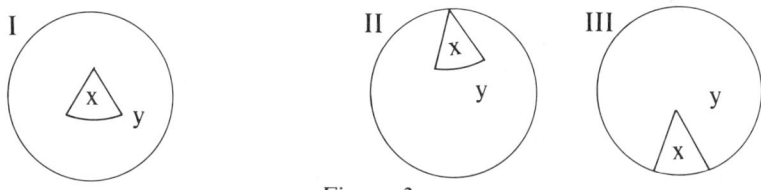

Figure 3

The properties of this relation will be adapted from those which characterize the notion of a 'neighborhood of a point' in a topological space. A number of modifications in the expression of these properties are required, however; first by the lack in *CI* of anything corresponding to the empty set, second by the need to replace set membership by the 'part of' relation, and finally by a difficulty in transplanting a distinction between finite and arbitrary unions and intersections which will be discussed below.

For *x,* a part of *y,* to lie on the inside of *y,* *x* must not 'touch' the outside of y. The first axiom acknowledges that nothing lies outside of *U* (the fusion of all Individuals)

$$\text{Ax 4} \quad (x)(x \lhd U).$$

As with the axioms and theorems of *CI,* the axioms of *CI*'s topology represent implicit rather than explicit and consciously employed principles. Axiom 5 describes one such principle, viz. that if *x* is interior to *y,* it is interior to everything of which *y* is a part. A corresponding principle, that if *x* is interior to *y,* every part of *x* is interior to *y,* follows from Axioms 5 and 6.

$$\text{Ax 5} \quad (x)(y)(z)(x \lhd y \,\&\, y \subseteq z \to x \lhd z),$$
$$\text{Ax 6} \quad (x)(y)(x \lhd y \to -y \lhd -x).$$

Because *separation* will be defined,

$$\text{Df 6} \quad x \, S \, y =_{df.} x \lhd -y,$$

and *connection* by

$$\text{Df } 7 \quad x \, c \, y = \text{df.} \sim (x \, S \, y),$$

Axiom 6 supplies the symmetry of these two relations.

The three axioms so far set down do not give any properties of $\lhd$ which distinguish it from $\subseteq$. One such is given by

$$\text{Ax } 7 \quad (x)(y)(x \neq U \, \& \, x \lhd y \rightarrow x \subseteq y).$$

Axioms 4 to 7 do not distinguish $\lhd$ from $\subseteq$; however, either of the next axioms will do this,

$$\text{Ax } 8 \quad (x)(y)(z)(w)(y \lhd x \, \& \, z \lhd x \, \& \, w \, \text{Fu}\{y, z\} \rightarrow w \lhd x).$$
$$\text{Ax } 9 \quad (x)(y)(z)(w)(x \lhd y \, \& \, x \lhd z \, \& \, w \, \text{Nu}\{y, z\} \rightarrow x \lhd w).$$

If the language user, whose mastery this structure represents, recognizes a distinction between II and III of figure 3, then the axioms as they stand do not distinguish the relation pictured in diagram II from $\lhd$ (pictured in diagram I). This could be done altering Ax 8 to read

$$\text{Ax } 8' \quad ((i)(i \, \varepsilon \, I \dashrightarrow x_i \lhd y) \rightarrow (z \, \text{Fu}\{x_i: i \, \varepsilon \, I\} \rightarrow z \lhd y)),$$

(where I is any set which can index the parts of y) for in II, y could equal a fusion of pie slices like x if there were one such slice for every point on the edge of y, hence the relationship pictured in this diagram would violate the extended Axiom 8 together with Axiom 7. The grasp of this distinction would then be reflected in the distinction between 'finite' and 'arbitrary' fusions.

Recognizing a distinction between II and III requires, in addition to freeing the determination of Individuals from actual features (e.g. adding the grasp of parts *potentially* determined by features), a grasp of mathematical idealization; II represents 'point contact' between x and the 'outside' of y. If our model language user is not to be considered sophisticated enough to deal with mathematical abstractions, we are not thereby required to think of him as a reactionary mathematician of the fourth century b.c. maintaining that all contact between bodies is 'surface contact'. For the unsophisticated the question does not arise, but the language user may still make judgements about interior and frontier parts. Apple pips are interior parts, the core and peel are frontier parts of the apple. It is this ability to distinguish between frontier and interior parts—and likewise between parts of the exterior which are connected and those which are separated from the object—which offers us more than a minimal account of what it is to be able to determine the limits or boundaries of objects.

It is not a drawback of the theoretical representation just outlined that it points the way to questions the language user may not have raised; rather, it is an advantage of the theory that it anticipates mathematical idealizations without presupposing a grasp of such abstractions. Consider an unsophisticated language user whose reports are implicitly governed by the principle, Ax 8, that a fusion of interior parts is an interior part. As long as he thinks in terms of finite fusions, what is left after such a fusion of interior parts is removed is a 'real' part of the object, a shell or rind. If his space is dense he may come to recognize that any such shell also contains parts which are interior to the original object. If he then raises the question, 'what is left over after *all possible* interior parts are removed?' (thereby removing the restriction of finitude from his quantifier), he will be led to the conception of an 'ideal skin', a mathematician's surface.

The extension of *CI* sketched above offers an attractive prospect to a philosopher who feels that one should in principle be able to analyse the notion of surface in terms of bodies or volumes (see Geach, 1969, pp. 69-70). What is required is an account of the identity of surfaces expressed in terms of the identity of bodies or volumes. To do this we will need to do more than assign an 'ideal skin' to every three dimensional object; not all surfaces, after all, are closed curves in space. A sufficiently general approach would be to say what it is for two pairs of (pair-wise) discrete objects to be in contact over the same surface.

To illustrate: the pair *AB* has between them the same boundary as the pair *CD* in (i) of figure 4, but not in (ii).

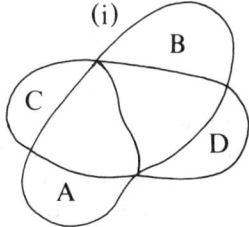 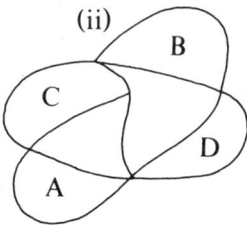

Figure 4

What is true of (i), but not of (ii) is that every part of *A* in contact with *B* overlaps *C*, every part of *C* in contact with *D* overlaps *A*, every part of *B* in contact with *A* overlaps *D* and every part of *D* in contact with *C* overlaps *B*. One of these four clauses is not true of figure (ii), for here is a part of *C* in contact with *D* which does not overlap *A*. It is not a straightforward matter to turn these observations into an adequate definition of identity for ideal boundaries, however, because of the possibility illustrated by (iii) (figure 5).

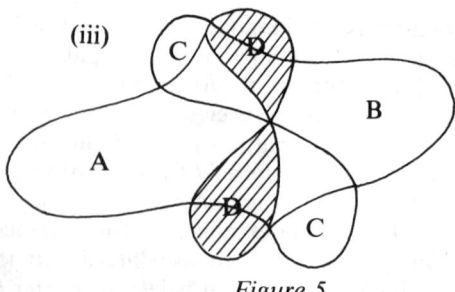

Figure 5

Here C and D each overlap both A and B, but nevertheless C and D have the same boundary between them as A and B. It is possible to state the definition in such a way as to accommodate cases such as (iii), but I will not pursue the development of this here.

Although it is a major strength of the extension of CI presented above that it suggests a philosophic foundation for ideal boundaries, its principal attraction here is that it offers a representation of the grasp of limits and boundaries of objects which does not require a grasp of ideal notions, but nevertheless leaves room for their addition. A second important attraction of this extension of CI is that it also affords a theoretical representation of the grasp of the limits and extent of objects whose boundaries are vague or imprecise. This is something with which language users cope everyday. We have, for example, no trouble locating and distinguishing hills and mountains, but sometimes have acute difficulties in saying exactly how far the slope of a given hill or mountain extends. In spite of these difficulties we can specify with complete confidence areas that clearly lie on the hill and areas within which the hill clearly lies. It may be obvious that Holmgill Knotts and Kirkfell Tarn lie on Wasdale Fell and that Wasdale Fell lies in the parish of Ennerdale and Kinniside, but it may be far from obvious *precisely* where Wasdale Fell begins and ends. Judgements of the sort which we can make with confidence may be represented by '$A \lhd B \lhd C$', but there may be many interior parts of C, C_i, for which we will not be confident of the truth of '$B \lhd C_i$' and many parts of C, A_j, such that we would be happy to affirm '$A \lhd A_j$', but uncertain whether '$A_j \lhd B$'. Agreement on a sufficiently wide range of such judgements, however, is enough to establish the possibility of communication.

One aim of extending CI was to capture the notion of self-connectedness. An Individual, A, is self-connected if for every pair A_1, A_2, such that A Fu$\{A_1, A_2\}$, either $A_1 o A_2$ or A_1 is connected to A_2 (i.e. $\sim (A_1 \lhd -A_2)$). A third attraction of the extended theory is that it also permits the representation of less strict connections. One could make use of such less strict connections in representing, say, our ability to distinguish three irregular clumps of trees in a field, determining the limits of each clump not by requiring the trees of one clump to touch one another, but only to be sufficiently close to one another. Connection based on proximity can be represented in *CI* by making stricter demands on the interior relation: *A* will not be judged to be interior to *B* unless the distance from any part of *A* to the exterior of *B* is greater than some fixed distance. Relying in this way on judgements of distance need not require mastery of sophisticated metric notions or principles but simply agreement on 'eyeball' judgements.

The possibility of varying in this way what is to count as being interior (and hence what is to count as being connected) arms us against the critic who would draw on sub-microscopic models of matter to argue that nothing is *really* self-connected, no two bodies *really* touch one another; they all ultimately consist of clouds of sub-atomic particles. Suppose on closer examination the three irregular clumps of trees mentioned above do turn out to be composed of trees not touching one another. The clumps remain distinguishable and their boundaries determinable to moderate precision. The judgements made in the closer examination can be represented by a stricter interior relation. In similar fashion we can represent the interior relation for ordinary material objects as requiring a gap perceptible without aid between interior part and the exterior of that of which it is a part. Unperceived discontinuities do not affect the way we distinguish objects.

Thus self-connectedness is not one principle of distinctness but the *form* of many principles, depending on the strictness of the interior and connection relations being used. This is an acceptable consequence, for it reflects our ability to see in the following figure two large clumps of dots each composed of three smaller clumps. Counting clumps will depend on a grasp of how close counts as 'connected'. Combining principles could yield a tally of eight or nine clumps in the figure, just as one may come up with the total of 204 squares on a chess board.

Figure 6

It should be clear from these considerations (as well as from the amount of theory required to express 'connectedness') that 'maximally self-connected region' deserves to be treated as a 'pattern for the occupation of space'. It is, thus, no objection to the letter of Strawson's claim—that 'snow', 'coal' and similar concepts do not by themselves provide a principle for distinguishing and counting particulars— that one could easily distinguish and count uninterrupted regions of snow or coal. On the other hand, self-connectedness *does* provide, if not a full principle of distinctness, at least the form of some such principles, and it is worth considering how it does so, and what this contributes to our understanding of such principles.

Section 9

The grasp of a principle of distinctness involves a grasp of what constitutes a complete instance. In some cases it is possible to distinguish incomplete instances, in other cases it is possible only to fail to distinguish completely.

One might advance the following thesis: the recognition of shapes or characteristic patterns in space or in time depends on a prior ability to pick out uniform regions or periods and hence on a grasp of the principle of distinctness based on uninterruptedness. This point does not turn on ignoring patterns which are composed of two or more disconnected parts (e.g. constellations) for it can be argued that such patterns must ultimately be composed of a number of maximally self-connected parts, otherwise how would it be possible to discern the pattern?

This thesis may amount to no more than the truism that recognition of any pattern depends on a contrast between figure and background. If it suggests further that a language user *may* learn to distinguish and count uninterrupted regions or periods before learning to do this with other characteristic patterns and *may* rely on the uninterruptedness, say, of a colour patch to isolate examples of triangles while someone teaches him the use of the word 'triangle'—all this is acceptable.

If, on the other hand, stress were laid on 'uniform' and an attempt made to argue that mass concepts (or feature concepts which correspond to mass words, including colour words) are necessarily the first concepts a language user must master, the thesis should be rejected. Learning what is to count as a uniform region or period may involve learning to ignore certain variations in hue, density, shine or shadow (see Anscombe 1964, p. 76 and M. Tiles 1974, pp. 61, 81), and thus depend on the isolation of a shape or pattern and accepting that what occurs within that region or period is uniformly ϕ. Pictures can be broken down into 'paint by number' mosaics only because human beings are already able to ignore such features as hue, shine or shadow.

The strong and unacceptable thesis being considered here is, when applied to the temporal dimension, the view that all events have to be seen as composed of elements whose identity depends on lack of change. Uniformity in the temporal realm is easily confused with lack of change, but a person (even a person thought of in terms of the feature placer) needs to be able to recognize and report neither change nor lack of change to be able to discriminate temporal patterns such as tone and rhythm phrases.

If this thesis is untenable in its strong form, what does uninterruptedness have to teach us about distinctness principles? Given that a language user is clear about what he is supposed to distinguish, consider the mistakes he might make: someone has failed properly to distinguish ϕs when he treats two or more ϕs as one or one ϕ as two or more. If the limits of one ϕ are determined by the uninterruptedness of ϕ, then the first mistake might well arise from failing to notice that the parts of what was taken as a single connected region are in fact not connected. The second mistake might arise from failing to notice where regions are connected.

If, on the other hand, the limits of one ϕ are to be determined by some other principle, then, obviously, it will be possible for instances of the pattern to share a common boundary, to overlap or intermingle (figure 7). Errors will not usually consist in mistaking part for whole or whole for part, but may nevertheless involve misjudgements about part-whole relations. In terms of figure 7, mistaking an arc for a circle shows a confusion about what is to be distinguished, but while possessing a grasp about what is to be distinguished, one might still err by assigning too many arcs to one circle, or by making out too many circles for the arcs present.

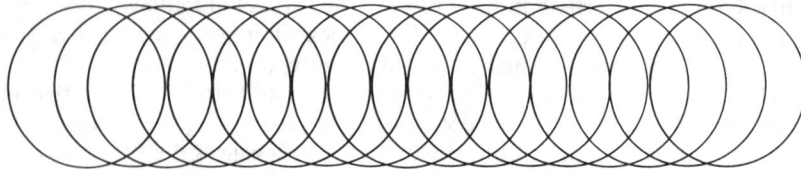

Figure 7

Recognition of mistakes in each of these cases requires a grasp of what is to count as (one) *complete* ϕ, and correctly distinguishing individual ϕs therefore involves what may be called a 'principle of completeness' for ϕ. So much is not a complete circle—it needs a bit like this attached to it. So much is more than a complete circle—this bit here should come off. So much is not a connected expanse of snow—there is more snow touching it here. So much is more than a connected expanse of snow—this part is not connected to the rest.

It might appear that the first model language user, the feature placer, already made use of principles of completeness, since in clarifying what it would be for him to use feature correlates of such concepts as *cat* it was said (above, p. 32) that he would respond with the feature word 'cat' only to the appearance of at least one complete cat. Being able to do this, however, does not amount to a grasp of what constitutes a complete cat, or even a complete catshape. The feature placer does not respond to incomplete cats as such. There is no connection between any response he may make to detached cat parts (or dismembered cats) and the response he makes to at least one whole cat.

His more advanced cousin, the feature Placer, uses his grasp of 'cat' to distinguish a Place (for a given time)—that place being all of his perceptual field taken up by complete cat-shapes—and he can distinguish parts of this cat-Place by means of feature concepts such as 'cat-face', 'ginger coloured', 'warm', etc. But this advanced cousin has no better grasp of principles of completeness. He does not relate detached cat parts to the cat-Place; he does not distinguish those parts of the cat-Place which constitute individual cat-Places. He can report that a fusion of Places is identical to the cat-Place, but not that a fusion of Places constitutes one individual cat-Place.

If these limitations to the feature Placer's abilities show he has no grasp of principles of completeness then it is clear what abilities he must acquire if he is to display a grasp of such principles. One thing it was pointed out that he cannot do is respond to detached or dismembered cats as such. A human being can come across a piece of wood and recognize it as an axe handle, a piece of window frame, a table leg. The rest of the axe, window frame, or table need not be present or ever have existed. Humans can also recognize activities such as digging (post) holes, moving a saw back and forth, stirring batter, as parts of events (erecting a fence, sawing a board in two, making a cake) which may never be complete (Kenny 1963, p. 174.) This recognition of unfinished, incomplete, or part objects or events displays a grasp of principles of what is to constitute complete objects or events.

So one way for a feature Placer to display his grasp of a principle of completeness would be for him to report on the presence, limits and extent of a Place or Time which, because it is distinguished by feature ψ, constitutes an unfinished, incomplete or part Place or Time as distinguished by ϕ. These reports would be made where ϕ does not in fact distinguish a finished, complete or whole Place or Time. Doing this would clearly reach beyond the resources of a language built on CI, for the relation between a 'part X' (in the sense of an incomplete X) and X cannot be expressed in terms of a relation which behaves like $\subseteq$ (which obtains only between actually distinguished Individuals).

This way of displaying a grasp of a principle of completeness does not, however, afford a way of displaying the grasp of the principle (or family of principles) associated with maximally connected regions (e.g. of snow or coal) or periods (of a glow or tone). It is not possible to encounter a *part* of such a region or period which is not *part of* a maximally connected region or period; maximal connection is not a principle which

provides a basis for the recognition of incomplete unfinished or part
Places or Times This observation takes us much closer to the heart of the
distinction which Strawson felt to exist between features which 'include
the idea' of a 'characteristic pattern' and those which do not. It is not
that the latter cannot be used to distinguish individual instances; it is that
such concepts do not enable a language user to recognize incomplete
instances, parts isolated from wholes.

This does not mean the principles derived from maximal connection
do not deserve to be thought of as principles of completeness. A feature
(shadow) may incompletely distinguish one connected ϕ-Place (e.g. the
snow-Place AB in figure 2); or it may distinguish one connected ϕ-Place
(B', same figure); or it may distinguish more than one connected ϕ-Place
(all of figure 2). A feature Placer can display a grasp of this kind of
completeness principle when he can say whether the part of $P(\phi)$ distinguished by some feature is *one* $P(\phi)$ and when it is not. This way of
displaying his grasp may also be used for principles associated with
features which 'include the idea of a characteristic pattern' as well as for
those which do not. If a feature Placer can display his grasp of
completeness principles in both of the ways discussed in this and the
preceding two paragraphs, he will also be able to display a grasp of the
distinction between feature concepts which include the 'characteristic
pattern' and those which do not.

An account has been given of what it would be to display a grasp of
principles of completeness, but apart from a few brief and inadequate
remarks no attempt will be made to describe the extended syntax a
feature Placer would need to make the required reports. What the
feature Placer requires by way of syntactic resources is the ability to form
complex general terms the application of which cannot be resolved into
the conjunction of the application of each constituent. To say of something that it is (a) red ball is to say it is (a) ball and red. The application
resolves into the application of the constituents of the complex. A
complex which cannot be so resolved is 'forged passport'; a forged
passport is forged, but is not a passport. ('Forged' is an example of a
logical attributive, see Lacey 1976, p. 11.) To report unfinished X,
incomplete X, or part X, a feature Placer will need to use complexes
which apply to what is not X.

The understanding and use of such complex phrases is clearly dependent on the understanding and use of their constituents, but cannot be
based completely on whatever grasp may be had of the constituents in
isolation. Something happens to the semantic powers[12] of the
constituents when they combine which can be compared to the change in
the powers of sodium and chlorine when they combine. This comparison

is more apt in cases where the constituents have an independent use, as in Quine's examples (1960, p. 103) 'water wings', 'water meters', 'water rights', 'water rats'. The constituents of some complexes do not have an independent use outside of some (sometimes only implicit) complex. 'Large', 'small', 'fake', 'forged', 'real,' 'genuine' are what Austin (1962, pp. 68-70) called 'substantive-hungry' expressions: to call something 'large', 'fake' or 'genuine' one must make clear or be prepared to make clear, 'large what?', 'fake what?', 'genuine what?'.

What is required of the feature Placer's use of 'complete', 'incomplete', 'part', 'whole', 'one', means that these words will not have an independent use outside of complex expressions and the contribution they make to a complex will be influenced by the other constituents of the complex. This is unlike any complex expression the feature Placer is so far able to use. His complex expressions are formed by means of the *Fu* and *Nu* operators. The applications of complexes formed using these operators are resolvable into conjunctions and disjunctions of the application of the constituents. There is no scope within the apparatus of *CI* to represent the sort of complexes required for the display of the grasp of principles of completeness.

It is widely acknowledged that complex expressions of the kind needed here have no satisfactory representation in semantic theories.[13] Although it would evidently strengthen and deepen the account of the grasp of principles of completeness if a satisfactory general representation of the use of such complex expressions could be drawn upon here, there is no room within the scope of this monograph to explore for new resources (outside semantic theory) or for new ways of exploiting old resources. The account as it stands is clear enough for us to continue to pursue an account of the grasp of principles of distinctness.

This and the previous section have uncovered resources which in the next section will be used to supplement the feature Placer's abilities so as to overcome those of his limitations which were highlighted in Section 7, especially the 'insufficient particularity' (p. 49) of Places and Times. Before turning to that task some remarks need to be made about the relation between part-whole judgements and identity principles— remarks which have in view the arguments to be used in Sections 12 and 15 of Chapter 3.

While the feature placer was unable to make judgements which permitted even the simplest quantificational complexity (p. 34), the feature Placer gained, along with the ability to make judgements whose logical structure was reflected in *CI,* the basis of an ability to apply more than one phrase to a single thing, Time or Place, as well as an ability to redescribe such things (p. 44). Nothing, thus, stood in the way of attributing quantifier complexity to the feature Placer's language, nor of saying that he possessed an ontology of Times and Places.

There is little doubt that the objects of this ontology are not at all what we are accustomed the think of as 'objects'—the problem of insufficient particularity makes that plain. Anyone who expected to arrive at some kind of 'genuine' or more familiar objects at the point identity principles first became available to our model language user is in danger of missing the lessons to be learned by considering what else besides fairly familiar objects can play certain logical roles. But someone prepared to enter the spirit of the present investigation might still feel that the principle that what has parts is an object cannot be used to support the claims of something to be a 'genuine' object. He might feel that redescription in terms of parts does not constitute a 'genuine' identity judgement. Chapter 3 will in two crucial sections (12 and 15) argue that because a creature must be able to redescribe an event in terms of events which are its constituent parts this creature must possess the grasp of a principle of identity for events. Resistance to using this principle must evidently be anticipated and having dwelt for four sections on various aspects of the mastery of the relation of part and whole, we can go some way to meeting it.

This resistance draws strength from the following consideration: surely there are uses of the notion of part and whole which are at best metaphorical, so that it takes more to show that genuine identity judgements are in play than the observation that a thing can be treated as having parts. One need only recall Plato's habit of speaking of the parts of the soul, or consider the possibility of treating the constituents of an emotion[14] as parts, to see how easy it is to use the metaphor.

It would be implausible to dismiss such examples by pointing to the difficulties one would have using them as the basis for an interpretation of *CI*. (How does one interpret the fusion of several souls?) A flexible imagination has to be used to incorporate familiar material bodies in interpretations of *CI*—recall the fusion of a writing instrument and a garden gate on p. 40, and one could easily devise arguably metaphorical interpretations of part and whole requiring no greater degree of imaginative flexibility than this. One could, for example, treat the rules of games as their parts, discover overlap between, say, field hockey and soccer, and allow artificial fusions, say, of the rules of bridge and chess to count as single Individuals.

The imaginative flexibility required for these interpretations stands as a clear indication of the limitations of *CI* as a tool for the analysis of our notion of part and whole. It is not that there is anything wrong with a logical tool which produces such unexpected objects; what is wrong is that the tool offers no resources for explaining why they should be unexpected. What is missing from *CI* became clearer in this section when the notion of a completeness principle was discussed. But the structure described by CI together with completeness principles do not show in what way the allegedly metaphorical uses of part and whole mentioned above are metaphorical.

Distinguishing precisely between strict and metaphorical usage is obviously frought with difficulty, but frequently one can point to classes of cases which must clearly be one rather than the other. I think it is reasonable to claim the the mastery of the topological relations of Section 8 equips a language user to discuss in fairly precise terms the limits and extent of any object to which the relations apply, and the ability to do this would seem clearly to amount to a grasp of a genuine principle of identity.

It would be ill-advised, and in any case it is unnecessary, to insist that the availability and mastery of such topological relations is a *necessary* condition for the possibility of genuine identity judgements. The arguments of Sections 12 and 15 require only that it be a sufficient condition. Maintaining this will by no means root out all the resistance to the arguments of those sections, but we are not yet in a position to examine closely what lies behind the word 'genuine', and this must wait until the concluding section.

Section 10

Sections 8 and 9 have located resources which overcome the crucial limitations observed in the model language user of Sections 5 and 6.

A feature Placer can display a grasp of a principle of completeness for ϕ if he is able to say when a feature ψ distinguishes a part of $P(\phi)$ or $T(\phi)$ (whichever is appropriate) which constitues one complete $P(\phi)$ or $T(\phi)$. For example, when ψ is *ginger*, and ϕ is *cat*, ψ distinguishes a complete part of $P(\text{cats})$ provided there is one all-ginger cat present. This seems, however, a fairly restricted application of what ought to be a powerful principle. There is no evidence in this performance of the use of a principle of completeness to *distinguish* a complete $P(\phi)$ or $T(\phi)$. Features are still relied upon entirely to distinguish the complete $P(\phi)$, i.e. the overlap of $P(\psi)$ and $P(\phi)$ (or $T(\psi)$ and $T(\phi)$) is distinguished by features ψ and ϕ and this is then judged to be or not to be a complete $P(\phi)$ (or $T(\phi)$). A principle of completeness ought nevertheless to be able to provide a principle for distinguishing Places and Times; it ought to be possible to use such a principle to distinguish one (complete) part of $P(\phi)$ without having to rely on features.

Suppose the overlap between $P(\psi)$ and $P(\phi)$ is not (and no part of it is) a complete $P(\phi)$: could not the principle of completeness be used to determine the limits and extent of that part of $P(\phi)$ of which $P(\psi)$ is a part and which constitutes a complete $P(\phi)$, *if there is one*? Suppose a feature Placer is faced with a number of cat-shapes, one of which is marked by one or several ginger spots, perhaps covering a small area of the shoulder or back leg, Could not a principle of what constitutes a complete cat-shape be used to determine the limits and extent of the one cat-shape which had ginger spots? There may, of course, be more than one such cat-shape (hence the clause, 'if there is one') and this allows some scope for a feature Placer to show his grasp of completeness as a principle for distinguishing Places. He can respond to questions of the form, 'Is $P(\text{ginger})$ part of *one* $P(\text{cats})$?'.

When a feature, ψ, (such as *ginger*) distinguishes a part of a Place $P(\phi)$(such as $P(\text{cats})$) which by itself does not constitute one or more complete $P(\phi)$, and instead the principle of completeness for $P(\phi)$ is used to distinguish a part of $P(\phi)$ consisting of one or more complete $P(\phi)$, the feature ψ will be called 'a mark'. There is, after all, no reason why marks should be used only to distinguish a Place consisting of at most one complete $P(\phi)$. If three of seven cat-shapes before a feature Placer had one or two ginger spots, the feature Placer could apply his grasp of what constitutes a complete cat-shape and distinguish that part of $P(\text{cats})$ which consists of the three cat-shapes marked by ginger.

Let this new way of distinguishing Places be represented by P(ginger/cats), or in general, $P(\psi/\phi)$, where the first feature provides the mark and the second feature the principles of completeness. It could be that all the cats present with ginger spots are also the cats with white spots (the rest being black, grey, etc.) The feature Placer can now use his principle of identity for Places to make reports of the form 'P(white/cat) = P(ginger/cat)'.

There is scope for marking complete $P(\phi)$s other than by means of features which distinguish parts of $P(\phi)$. The grasp of topological relations can be brought into play here. Of seven all black cat-shapes before the feature Placer, two may be lying on the edge of a piece of bright green felt. The topological relation between P(cats) and P(green) is expressed by 'P(cats) c P(green)', but it is only a two cat-shape part of P(cats) which touches P(green). The principle of completeness for cat-shape may, thus, be used to distinguish the two complete cat-shapes which are in contact with P(green). 'Contact with P(green)' thus functions like 'having a ginger part' and marks complete cats.[15]

The ability to use marks based on topological relations increases the number of situations in which a feature Placer can exercise his grasp of principles of completeness in order to distinguish Places. The interest in this new kind of mark does not, however, stop there. If we return to the possibility first canvassed on p. 46 of using the principle of identity for Places, (*), of CI as a principle of reidentification, we see that since topological relations between Places can alter without affecting the $\subseteq$ relations between Places it is possible to use this principle in the reidentification of Place $through\ changes$ in such relations. For example, two discrete Places can change from being separated to being in contact or $vice\ versa$ without altering any $\subseteq$ relations, or a Place can alter from being an interior part to being a frontier part of another Place without altering any $\subseteq$ relations.

The importance of this is that a feature Placer could (if equipped with all the rest of what is needed for a grasp of change) act on request to alter the topological relations between the Places he confronts in order to display his grasp of distinctness based on completeness. He could, in other words, act to mark all the complete $P(\phi)$s before him in a different way. But he can do this only using marks based on topological relations, for if he brings it about that features distinguish new parts of the $P(\phi)$ before him, ϕ no longer distinguishes the same Place it did before the marks were introduced. The best he can do is report on the distinct $P(\phi)$s of the new Place.

When the possibility of using the principle drawn from CI was first canvassed, it was pointed out that the feature Placer was unable to

distinguish times sufficiently to say whether the Place distinguished by a
feature ϕ at one time was or was not the same Place as that distinguished
by ϕ at another time. We must now see if sufficient resources are at hand
at least for the feature Placer to cope with an expanding experience.

The root of the problem which appeared on pp. 48-49 was the way
Times depended on features for their distinctness. This meant that no
Time was distinguished in such a way that a feature Placer could not
re-encounter that same Time. Moreover, since there was no way for
him to distinguish encounters with the same (temporal) disposition of
features there was no way for the feature Placer to display a grasp of
the fact that he *had* re-encountered the same Time. In the intervening
pages new resources for distinguishing Places and Times have been
developed; the feature Placer now has two kinds of principles of
completeness (based on maximal connection and on characteristic
patterns) which can be used to distinguish parts of a Time such as $T(\phi)$.
But it would seem upon reflection that these new resources do not
touch the root of the problem.

Before the addition of principles of completeness, distinct parts of
$T(\phi)$ could be distinguished only by distinct features. The distinct
features were required to determine the limits and extent of the distinct
parts. A principle (the *same* principle) of completeness for $T(\phi)$ can now
be used to determine the limits and extent of distinct parts of $T(\phi)$, but
only if the parts of $T(\phi)$ are distinctly marked in some way. If more than
one complete $T(\phi)$ is marked by some feature, ψ, $T(\psi/\phi)$ will be the part
of $T(\phi)$ consisting of all the complete $T(\phi)$s so marked, (likewise for
marks based on topological relations) and if these complete $T(\phi)$s are to
be distinguished it will have to be by means of other marks. Complete
$T(\phi)$s all marked in all the same way are distinguished as one, not further
subdistinguished, part of $T(\phi)$.

Times thus continue to be distinguished in such a way that it is possible
for the feature Placer to re-encounter the same Time and not be able to
distinguish his encounters. True, there are now many more ways for the
feature Placer to distinguish Times, but it remains possible in the extreme
case, for the whole of his temporally structured experience to repeat
itself, precisely, in every detail, and for those repetitions thus to count as
undistinguished parts of the same Time. Have we overlooked any way of
exploiting our new resources?

The feature Placer *can* say whether such a part of $T(\phi)$ is *one* or *not
one* (because more than one) complete $T(\phi)$, but to do this is not necessarily to display a grasp of the distinctness of the undistinguished $T(\phi)$s,
when the part of $T(\phi)$ thus distinguished is *not one*. Clear evidence of
that grasp comes when the feature Placer can report the correct number

of complete $T(\phi)$s. But, surely, in order to enumerate $T(\phi)$s is it not necessary to regard them as distinct? That is precisely the problem we face here: what is it for the feature Placer to regard $T(\phi)$s, undistinguished by marks of any kind, as distinct? And why should this prove any more difficult for a feature Placer than for us? In the extreme case we too are threatened by a complete repetition of our experience; how is it *we* are able to conceive the distinction required to imagine this possibility?

Let us look more closely at what is required if a feature Placer is successfully to enumerate $T(\phi)$s. At each step of the enumeration procedure he has to know which numeral to use next. There is here a separable ability he could acquire, one independent of his use of numerals to count any kind of Places or Times. Children can be taught to rattle off an initial segment of the numerals without learning to apply them to anything. Benacerraf aptly calls this unapplied recitation of the numerals 'intransitive counting' while the procedure of applying the numerals to events or objects is called 'transitive counting' (1965, p. 49). Suppose the feature Placer can recite an initial segment of the numerals in the correct order, postponing for a while the question of how high his segment needs to go. The feature Placer would then be able to count transitively if he could co-ordinate the performance of intransitive counting with a grasp of a principle of temporal completeness. At the sound of a uniform tone or the beginning of a characteristic tone phrase he readies the first word in his numeral series and as soon as the tone is interrupted by silence or the phrase ends, he recites his first word. When the tone or phrase begins again he readies his second word, and so on.

Success here seems possible without the uniform tones or repeated phrases needing to be distinguished by marks of any kind; in fact the recitation of the series provides the marks. The feature Placer's voice distinguishes Times which mark what may otherwise be unmarked $T(\phi)$s. The problem of how a feature Placer grasps the distinctness of undistinguished Times is circumvented by equipping him to *impose* distinguishing marks by a procedure which relies upon and further displays his grasp of principles of completeness.

The only threat to this way around the problem lies in the possibility that the initial segment of the numerals which the feature Placer can recite will be more than exhausted by a series of exactly similar $T(\phi)$s. If he runs out of distinguishing marks, he can only start over and then he has not succeeded in distinguishing the left-overs from those first $T(\phi)$s he counted. The possibility is evidently forestalled if the feature Placer has the ability to recite an unlimited series of numerals. But this, it may be objected, is to require an ability which the feature Placer will not be able to display. No matter how much of his numeral series we get him to recite there is no guarantee he will not at some point run out of new numerals.

This objection cannot be pressed too far without calling into question the belief that our own species possesses a grasp of an unlimited series of numerals, and in any case this is not the point at which to raise difficulties of this kind. All the abilities we have attributed to the feature Placer are in a sense unlimited. The ability always to respond to feature ϕ by producing the appropriate sign for ϕ cannot be completely manifested; all we could have on which to attribute this ability is success in a finite number of responses to ϕ. Still an ability to generate an unlimited series of mutually distinct objects ('words') is not the same sort of thing as the unlimited ability to respond to the same thing in the same way. Can anything be said about what the former ability involves?

It is clear that the feature Placer will have to be able to recite at least a finite ordered list of words correctly (say, for example, a list of five words: A, B, C, D, E). The first step in turning this into the mastery of an unlimited series would be for the feature Placer to learn to use his series to count his own recitations of the series. Leaving one recitation unmarked, he marks each word in the next recitation by the first word from his series, each word in the third recitation by the second, and so on:

$$A,B,C,D,E,AA,AB,AC,AD,AE,BA,BB,BC,BD,BE,CA,CB,CC,\ldots$$

When he runs out of words with which to mark his recitation, the next step is to count his countings of his recitations. The first counting of the recitations has been unmarked, each word of the next will be marked by the first word of the series, and so on:

$$\ldots AAA,AAB,AAC,\ldots ABA,ABB,ABC,\ldots\ \ \ldots BAA,BAB,\ldots^{16}$$

On this basis (which amounts to understanding the use of a successor operator) the feature Placer can be equipped with an understanding of a linear order relation 'precedes' on his numeral series. Roughly expressed, 'm precedes n' if and only if by reciting the series beginning at m, one will reach n. Precise formal representations of how the order relation rests on the successor operator are familiar and can be found in expositions of the foundations of arithmetic, (Dedekind 1963, pp. 44-115; Frege, 1950, esp. §79, 1964, esp. §45). The grasp of a temporal ordering relation on particular (complete) $T(\phi)$s can then be explained in terms of the order on the marks which are imposed on the $T(\phi)$s if they are enumerated correctly.

Once this temporal structure is within his grasp, a feature Placer may be said to be equipped to deal with an expanding experience. Is he now also able to make sufficient distinctions to apply a principle of reidentification? Strawson saw the idea of borrowing criteria of distinctness for Places from features as limited by lack of resources 'for conveying the identity of particulars through time' (1963, p. 227; above, pp. 45ff). The approach taken in Section 7 did suggest resources for reidentification, namely to apply the principle,

(*) $$(x)(y)((z)(z \subseteq x \leftrightarrow z \subseteq y \rightarrow x = y))$$

to Places encountered at different times. This suggestion faced two difficulties: (1) the Place distinguished by a feature might be different at different times and (2) the feature Placer could not distinguish times sufficiently to have a use for the above principle. Do the developments of the intervening pages provide resources for overcoming these difficulties?

The resources are there if the feature Placer can coordinate his abilities in a somewhat more complicated enumeration procedure. The feature Placer readies his first numeral when ϕ determines a Place in his perceptual field and recites it either when ϕ distinguishes a different Place (because of an alteration in the disposition of features in his field), or ϕ ceases to distinguish a Place (because he no longer experiences ϕ). If the first happens then he readies his second numeral and recites it when ϕ distinguishes a different Place or ceases to distinguish a Place. If the second happens he does not ready his second numeral until ϕ once again distinguishes a Place and then recites it when ϕ distinguishes a different Place or ceases to distinguish a Place. And so on for the numerals in succession. Let the results of this procedure be represented by $P(\phi)_1$, $P(\phi)_2$, $P(\phi)_3$, . . .

To avoid further complications in the description of this enumeration let us set aside the feature Placer's ability to apply a principle of spatial completeness in connection with $P(\phi)$, thereby distinguishing different $P(\phi)$s by means of marks. What are being counted, then in this procedure are, in effect, spells during which '$P(\phi)$' unambiguously determines a Place. These spells will be referred to hereafter as 'Place-encounters'. A feature Placer can apply his principle of reidentification for Places and on this basis report when two Place encounters are encounters with the same Place, e.g. he can report '$P(\phi)_i = P(\phi)_k$'. It remains possible for the same Place to be distinguished by distinct features or to be redescribed as a nucleus or fusion of Places.

A feature Placer is thus a model language user with a grasp of a principle of identity which includes the possibility of reidentification. This is not an adequate theoretical representation of our own linguistic mastery, but there is much to be learned from the limitations of such a model as a language user. The use to which he will be put in the next chapter is the clarification of the issues surrounding Strawson's position on events and basic particulars.

3

A Society of Feature Placers

Section 11
The model language user of Chapter II can be used to clarify the issues which surround Strawson's position on events vis-à-vis basic particulars.

The ability to distinguish Place-encounters, introduced at the end of the last chapter, opens new possibilities for distinguishing Times. Hitherto we have followed the suggestion that the criteria of distinctness for Times, as well as for Places, should be borrowed from features. Accordingly the limits of a Time are determined either by the occurrence of a temporal pattern feature or by the continuous presence of a temporally unstructured feature. Times could now equally easily be distinguished by Place-encounters, i.e. by the continuous unambiguous determination of a Place by a feature or combination of features. The Time distinguished by the presence of ϕ might have several parts distinguished by encounters with Places distinguished by ϕ. Let us represent the Times distinguished by Places in this way by allowing $P(\phi)_i$ (where i is any numeral) to act as an argument of $T(\ \ )$, just as features now do. Thus $T(P(\phi)_i)$ is the Time distinguished as the ith occasion ϕ distinguishes a Place. The grasp of the limits and extent of these Times will be displayed as before in the reports about the relations between parts and whole, interior and frontier parts, separation and connection.

An important difference between Times distinguished by features (as hitherto) and Times distinguished by Place-encounters is that the former are independent particulars while the latter are dependent particulars. Times cannot be distinguished by Place-encounters without a grasp of the principle of identity for Places. On the other hand a feature Placer need not use Place-encounters to distinguish Times. His grasp of the distinctness of Place-encounters is displayed by his correctly counting them. He does not, in fact, have to distinguish Times at all in order to make use of his principles for reidentifying Places. These observations clearly bear on Strawson's position vis-à-vis events and basic particulars, but before exploring their implications it will be worthwhile making a quick survey of a variety of dependent particulars which a feature Placer may add to his temporal concepts alongside Times distinguished by Place-encounters.

A feature Placer is able to report on topological relations between Places which may change without affecting the identity of Places. For example, if A and B are discrete Places, they may at one time be in contact and at another time be separated. In addition to distinguishing Times by means of features and by means of Place-encounters, a feature Placer might also distinguish the Time during which discrete Places A and B were in contact and the Time during which they were separated.

Again this new way of distinguishing Times may be represented by extending the arguments allowable in the $T(\ )$ operator, this time to include sentences which report these topological relations. For example $T(A \underline{c} B)$ would be the Time during which Places A and B were touching each other in the feature Placer's field. Let any Time distinguished by a report expressing a topological relation be called a 'State'. Distinguishing States evidently requires a grasp of the principle of identity for Places, so States are dependent particulars, just as were Times distinguished by Place-encounters. It is obvious that a feature Placer could make reports about topological relations between Places without using these reports to distinguish Times.

Suppose, nevertheless, that a feature Placer does distinguish States and, as before, A and B are discrete Places. So long as both Places are present in a feature Placer's perceptual field they are either separated or in contact. There is no part of the Time determined by the presence of both A and B which is not part of the fusion of the two non-overlapping States distinguished by contact and separation. Within the Time distinguished by the presence of both A and B in the feature Placer's perceptual field all boundaries between these States are ideal boundaries (see pp. 55ff.); any such ideal boundary will be called a 'Change'. If the feature Placer were equipped with a grasp of the principle of identity of ideal temporal boundaries we could say he had a grasp of the identity of (instantaneous) Changes. Clearly such Changes would be particulars dependent on a grasp of the identity of Places. A feature Placer could, however, *respond* to changes in topological relations between Places—by uttering a report which was correct to make only immediately after such a change had taken place—without needing to make use of a grasp of the identity of Changes.

For a notion related in an important way to 'Change', consider first the defined topological relation

Df 8   A ⊗ B $=_{df.}$ A ⊲ Fu{A, B} (read, '*A* is surrounded by *B*')

This is a relation which may obtain between discrete Places. It is not possible for '*A* ⊗ *B*' and '*A* *S* *B*' to be correct reports at the same time, but it is possible for neither to be correct although both *A* and *B* are present. Thus some parts of the Time distinguished by the presence of both *A* and *B* in the feature Placer's perceptual field might not be parts of the fusion of the two States T(A *S* B) and T(A ⊗ B).

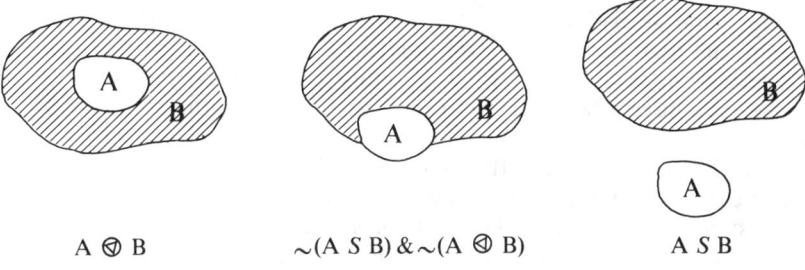

A ⊗ B   ~(A *S* B) & ~(A ⊗ B)   A *S* B

Figure 1

Any part of the Time determined by the presence of both *A* and *B* which falls between these two States will be called a 'transition State'.[1] It is clear that transition States are also dependent particulars, and again it is possible for a feature Placer to respond to a transition in which *A* moves from being surrounded by *B* to being separated from *B*, without needing to be able to distinguish the Times between which *A* ceased to be surrounded by *B* and became separated from *B*.

To spell out the implications of this for Strawson's position on events and basic particulars consider first the feature Placer who is equipped to enumerate Place-encounters, to report topological relations between Places and to respond to changes in those relations, but who uses none of these to distinguish Times. If (an important 'if') Places would serve as basic particulars, this model language user would embody precisely that separation of linguistic abilities which became an isssue at the end of Chapter 1. This feature Placer requires no dependent temporal particulars but is nevertheless able to respond to or report such relations and changes in his basic particulars as could be used to distinguish dependent particulars. This feature Placer represents the separability of the first and second levels of Strawson's stratification (above, pp. 26-27), just as the feature placer represented the separability of the ground and first levels.

To be sure it is most unlikely that Strawson would regard Places as an adequate set of basic particulars, but before seeing why, consider this objection: Places cannot be the only things in a feature Placer's ontology, for we have just seen that in order to reidentify Places a feature Placer has to be able to distinguish Place-encounters; there is no reidentification without this. This may be thought to reveal a constraint on Strawson's position as well (compare this to Moravcsik's objection to Strawson, above, p. 24.): whatever may be the claim Strawson makes for material bodies as basic particulars it cannot be the claim that material bodies are the *only* particulars we need (to do whatever concepts of material bodies are required to do) since we cannot reidentify material bodies without distinguishing our encounters with them. There are two things that need to be said to this objection, (1) it is not clear that feature Placers, so described, have what amounts to the grasp of the identity of Place-encounters, (2) it is far from clear that Strawson wants to claim what according to this he is unable to claim.

The first raises some difficult points. The feature Placer displays a grasp of the temporal limits and extent of Place encounters only insofar as he comes out with another numeral at the right moment. He cannot discuss the temporal parts of Place-encounters or of the Times they determine; he cannot redescribe either encounter or its Time in terms of its parts. The best he can do is to redescribe a Place encounter in terms of its numeral, e.g. the third $P(\phi)$ encounter after $P(\phi)_4$ is the fourth encounter before $P(\phi)_{11}$. But this requires an arithmetical sophistication which is not required in order to enumerate correctly, and hence is not needed in order to distinguish Place-encounters. The grasp of a successor function does not require the grasp of the arithmetical operations which may be defined in terms of it.

If Strawson were defending the absolute self-sufficiency of material bodies as a class of basic particulars we could offer him an argument along these lines as a defence against the need for a grasp of the identity of material-body-encounters. But owing to a certain elusiveness in the claims he makes on behalf of material bodies, it is not clear Strawson would want or need this argument. The claims seem straightforward enough: in order to refer identifyingly when communicating with others, we need a comprehensive framework in which 'each element is uniquely related to every other and hence to ourselves and our surroundings' (1963, p. 12). Material bodies give us that framework. Other categories are shown not to provide the framework because of their identification dependence on material bodies and presumably material bodies would be disqualified as basic if they could be shown to be dependent in this way on some other category. Unless, of course, that category is dependent on material bodies in turn and the two interdependent categories are not in turn dependent on something more basic. Should this happen it would seem that the claim must be expressed in terms of basic particulars including material bodies *and something else.*

As Strawson explicitly acknowledges, this is precisely the situation vis-à-vis places,

> So the identification and distinction of places turn on the identification and distinction of things; and the identification and distinction of things turn, in part, on the identification and distinction of places. (1963, p. 26)

It would seem from this that Strawson should be careful to say that basic particulars are material bodies plus places, but places are for some reason continually slighted.[2] In an effort to follow the spirit of Strawson's discussion, if not the letter, we might take 'basic particulars' as implicitly including all ancillary categories on which material bodies depend for their identification, such as places and presumably (from the emphasis on a spatio-*temporal* framework) times. If it is successfully shown that this dependence extends to body-encounters and place-encounters (remembering that has not been convincingly argued) then these too should be regarded as falling under the rubric, 'basic particulars'.

This generous reading of 'basic particulars' could in turn be applied to the category of events. The natural first reaction of the philosophically refined intuition (witness Davidson and Moravcsik) is that there must be at least as much mutual dependence between bodies and events as between bodies and places. But here we face Strawson's arguments to the contrary (examined and reconstructed, above, pp. 13ff.); in the context of discussing basic particulars he argues that one could do without 'events, processes, states and conditions' (1963, p. 43). Looked at from the standpoint of the separability of certain parts of the mastery of our language, this position has withstood considerable critical pressure. Now, however, we are approaching it with a wider range of demands. How, for a start, is the temporal dimension of the unified spatio-temporal framework to be constituted without relying on events, states, or processes?

There is no hint that the spatio-temporal framework can be used without a grasp of the distinctness and identity of particular *times*, so we may include them under 'basic particulars' with as much justification as we include places. The crucial question is how times are to be distinguished. If they rely on events, states or processes, Strawson's position will collapse. The model of the feature Placer will help to clarify the options: his Times need not be distinguished by relations or transitions

between Places; he might rely only on features to distinguish Times.
(Doing this would correspond to using spells of light and dark, warmth
and cold, etc. to distinguish times.) He need not rely directly on features,
but instead use only Place-encounters to distinguish all his Times.

Strawson might be maintaining that a temporal framework of sufficient complexity could conceivably be constituted by the relations
between times whose distinctness is 'borrowed' from something like
feature concepts—or, perhaps, 'borrowed' only from encounters with
material bodies and places. The second of these might well be the way we
should interpret Strawson's all too brief treatment of these matters,

> The fact that identification in general has a temporal as well as a spatial
> aspect is no objection. For material bodies, or things which have them,
> exhibit relations between themselves which have temporal aspect. One
> thing replaces or begets another. Things pass through places. (1963, p. 45)

But the illustrations seem to point in another direction.

Perhaps Strawson would allow not only encounters to determine times
but also events (begettings, replacements) including processes (passages
through a place) and deny that for one to use such things to distinguish
times it is necessary to possess a grasp of the identity of particular events
or processes. Here again the position of the feature Placer may be used to
clarify the situation: when the feature Placer distinguishes and
redescribes States, transition States and Changes, this does not
correspond to a grasp of particular states or events such as might find a
place in our conceptual abilities. Such particulars do not correspond to
John's spending the day in bed, Peter's trip to London, or Mary's arrival
home. They correspond to the time John spent in bed, the time Peter
spent travelling to London (these two might be identical) or the time
Mary arrived home. They correspond to last month, the season between
winter and summer, the beginning of the year.

This can be brought out further by considering the possibilities for
redescription. Suppose that as Peter boarded a train in Bristol, John lay
down for a nap (in Dorking) and, at the moment he arose, Mary started
preparing supper (in Poole) and finished just as Peter arrived in London.
We can redescribe the *time* of Peter's trip in terms of John's nap and
Mary's work in the kitchen, but we cannot redescribe Peter's *trip* in this
way. The feature Placer does not redescribe states or transitions; States
and transition States are Times and his ability to redescribe them rests on
the level of a redescription of the *time* of Peter's trip, not his *trip*.

We might, nevertheless, use the *time* of John's nap to distinguish a
part of Peter's trip, viz. that part of the trip which took precisely the time
John's nap took. To do this is to determine a part of Peter's trip

indirectly. To determine a part of Peter's trip *directly* one would have to make use of something like the leg of the journey from Chippenham to Didcot. Evidence of a grasp of the identity of particular events as opposed to particular times would be the use of a distinction between direct and indirect determination of the parts of temporal items. The feature Placer does not make use of such a distinction vis-à-vis Times.

It may be that Strawson's position is this: it would be possible to borrow criteria of distinctness for times from reports to the effect that so and so is in such and such a place (or condition), or passing through such and such a place (or condition), without needing a grasp of the identity of events or states. This version of the position has the advantage that the temporal dimension of the framework of reference is very likely to be as rich in particular times as one could ask. So distinguished and redescribable, times would be dependent particulars (dependent on both bodies and places), and like places would be *interdependent*. But this would not undermine what Strawson says about events, processes, states and conditions, since no grasp of a principle of identity for such things is required to distinguish and reidentify times.

The aim of this chapter is to show that a grasp of the kind of framework which Strawson says is required for identifying reference depends on the ability directly to distinguish the parts of the movements of bodies (or at least of place occupiers) and also to be able to redescribe movements in terms of their directly determined parts. If this can be shown, then it does not matter which of the positions just outlined is Strawson's, whether he envisages the distinctness of times as relying only on body and place encounters, or whether they can also be determined by reports of states, processes, etc. If this can be shown, Strawson cannot claim the grasp of the identity of bodies (or, at least, place occupiers) is independent of the grasp of the identity of events or processes.

Section 12
A community whose members conceived of changes in their own
position would need to use a principle of identity for events.

Evidently a great deal will turn on what Strawson says is required of a set
of basic particulars. In an effort to clarify this it would be helpful to ask
why Places would not serve the feature Placer as a set of basic particulars. Places are obviously not what we would think of as material
bodies, but Strawson does not insist that only what we would think of as
material bodies will serve as basic particulars. He is prepared to allow the
possibility that 'purely visual three dimensional objects' (1963, p. 30)
would also do. The feature Placer's various perceptual organs are
integrated into a single perceptual field like a visual field, but his limited
spatial concepts hardly support a grasp of dimensionality. On the other
hand, it is far from clear what this precise number of dimensions—or
dimensionality in general—contributes to the role of a spatial framework
in making possible identifying reference.

Basic particulars require, according to Strawson,

> enough diversity, richness, stability and endurance to make possible and
> natural just that conception of a single unitary framework which we
> possess. (*ibid.,* pp. 28-9)

Suppose a feature Placer were equipped with roughly our sensory
capacities, placed in our world and required to use his grasp of 'Place' to
respond to what we think of as material bodies. His 'Places' might well
prove as stable and durable as our 'material bodies', but for one
important difficulty. We conceive of material bodies as enduring when
we are not perceiving them—indeed when no one is perceiving them.
When a feature Placer no longer confronts a Place, that Place no longer
exists for him. That same Place might reappear later, but it has not, for
him, persisted somewhere else; there is nowhere outside his experience
for that Place to be. It is this difficulty which, more than anything,
would disqualify Places as candidates for basic particulars.

It is not difficult to see why the conception of particulars which can
exist when not personally encountered is important in communication.
In order to communicate, a creature must be able to interpret the
utterances of other creatures whose experience differs from his own. A
feature Placer functioning in a community of feature Placers must be
able to accept a report about a Place which he is not at that moment
encountering and thus locate that Place somewhere—'locate', that is, in
a loose sense, perhaps only 'in that other Placer's experience'. A feature

Placer able to send, receive and collate reports from other creatures with comparable linguistic abilities will display a grasp of a framework which includes, at least, more than his own experience.

Before examining how the demands of communication might constrain the structure of that framework, it is advisable to consider another important use to which a spatial framework may be put. Another use might well impose its own constraints on the nature and structure of that framework. Since we are concerned primarily with the constraints imposed by the demands of identifying reference, we will want to keep other constraints separate from these.

A creature who acts to affect what he experiences by moving himself about, could use a spatial framework in the co-ordination of his action and experience. One can understand this use and how it might constrain a framework if one first imagines a creature whose movements recall the Arabian Nights: the press of a button or the whisper of a magic word whisks him from, e.g., Anchorage to Istanbul. If this kind of instantaneous movement is *all* the movement he knows, his space need have no more structure than a set of discrete unrelated objects. He needs no grasp of any geographical relations between Anchorage and Istanbul to find the right button or word.

Another creature who moves himself in an equally mysterious manner might find his movements restricted in various ways. He cannot 'whisk' himself from A to D; to get from A to D he has first to press the right button to get from A to B, then a button to get from B to C and finally one to get from C to D. He might then find that to get back to A he has to reverse the procedure going via C and B (a linearly ordered space) or he might be able to get to A directly from D (circular space.) This creature's spatial framework will be structured by the routes he is constrained to take. We are, as a matter of fact, free to move between two places by an indefinitely large number of routes, but are also, as a matter of fact, constrained to follow some route or other. We cannot travel between Anchorage and Istanbul without going through other places; no road leads only to Rome.

Between the linear space and our own there are a number of possible spaces. One space it is instructive to consider is one whose places and routes are isomorphic to the distribution of stations and lines of the London Underground. No traveller negotiating the Underground is compelled to relate stations in any way other than along the paths the trains follow (e.g. take account of the fact that station X is three miles northwest of station Y and that the line takes in several stations northeast and due north of Y along a six mile path). He needs, however, a mastery of the system (represented on the familiar schematic map) in order to get on a train going in the right direction, monitor his progress, get off on the right platform, change to the right line, get on a train going in the right direction, monitor his progress and get off at his destination.

A creature—even one who moves by magic words or buttons—who has to monitor his progress so as to act correctly at certain points along his route in order to reach his destination will have to be able to relate parts of his journey to the whole of it. This fact is likely to obscure the issue of whether it is possible for a set of particulars to constitute an adequate spatio-temporal framework without including elements from Strawson's list of dispensable particulars; events, processes, states or conditions.

To see why, consider what is involved in integrating this ability with the ability to communicate with similar creatures. Such an integration would involve our mobile creatures in the activities of issuing and accepting instructions to move from place to place, reporting the progress and completion of their movements and interpreting the reports of others in the light of their movements. This requires of each member of the community a grasp of what it is for one of their number to occupy distinct places and of the transition between those places.

These creatures (imagine their space at least as complex as the London Underground System) are not to be thought of as feature Placers, but it is important to ask if their grasp of position and transition could exist on the level at which a feature Placer reports on topological relations and responds to transitions between such relations. The significant point here is that a feature Placer did not have to possess even a grasp of the limits and extent of *transition States,* did not have to distinguish their parts or to redescribe them in terms of their parts, but a creature able to monitor and interpret reports in the light of progress along a transition route will have to distinguish parts *of a transition,* and redescribe that transition in terms of transitions which form its parts. He requires, in other words, a grasp of the very kind of dependent particulars which Strawson claimed were not needed in a set of basic particulars.

He requires this, however, in order to be able to discuss with other members of his community movements in a space where movers are constrained to follow routes. This establishes merely that he needs such a grasp if he is to communicate about certain matters, not that he needs such a grasp if his communications are to involve identifying references. This exposes a hazard. To argue that a language community requires events or processes in its set of basic particulars if its framework is to be adequate to cope with the movements of members of the community is to fail to engage Strawson's thesis. The spatio-temporal framework which basic particulars are to provide does not have to cope only with every demand which might be made on such a framework; it must cope with the demands imposed by the possibility of identifying reference.

To avoid this hazard the present investigation will concentrate on the requirements of a community of sentient trees which are each rooted in one spot and thus have no need for a conception of the change of position of their comrades. As we already have a model language user whose principles of identity do not provide him with basic particulars, we can proceed by asking what elaborations in the feature Placer's abilities are required if he is to function as a member of such a community of sentient trees. This will, of course, leave the investigation on the artificial plane it has occupied since the beginning of Chapter 2, but there is considerable advantage to be gained in this case. We may leave out of our discussion the complexities introduced by the need of one member of a language community to interpret the reports of other members in the light of their positions. The representation of the community's framework can thus be simplified by identifying position ('place' in a more literal sense than is captured by 'Place') with members' viewpoints or perceptual fields. What this involves will be spelled out in Section 14.

A community which does not conceive of the movements of its members is not barred from a conception of the movements of things through its midst. Reports exchanged by members of the community moreover could, we have seen, embody responses to such movements without the community needing to distinguish or redescribe movements. What would refute Strawson's position, at least vis-à-vis events or processes, would be an argument to show that to possess an adequate spatio-temporal framework the community *must* distinguish and redescribe the movements of things through its midst.

This is what the remainder of this chapter will be devoted to showing, but because we must first examine in more detail the demands Strawson makes on basic particulars vis-à-vis the framework of reference (and also consider the extent to which these demands can be met without the grasp of identity principles for the particular movements of things) it will be easy to loose sight of the overall strategy of this Chapter. The strategy has the form of a dilemma: either the members of a linguistic community will, in order to possess a common framework of reference, have to conceive of their movements within that framework, or they will not. This section has argued that if they must conceive of their own movements they will require principles of identity for particualr movements. Section 15 will argue that if they do not have to conceive of thier own movements, they will still require the grasp of a principle of identity for particular movements.

Section 13
It is not impossible for a language community to operate with a spatio-temporal framework which is unified temporally but not spatially. Such a community would, naturally, not be able to do many things with their language which humans are able to do.

Strawson was quoted above as insisting that basic particulars must have,

> enough diversity, richness, stability and endurance to make possible and natural just that conception of a single unitary framework which we possess. (1963, pp. 28-9)

As the unity of the spatio-temporal framework will be the crux of the argument of this chapter, we must come to an understanding of the motivation and status of this requirement, for Strawson gives us no precise statement of what that unity is to consist in. Even one point on which Strawson seems clear—the framework cannot have only a temporal unity—is hedged in almost to extinction.

The sort of framework Strawson has in mind as inadequate is one based on 'directly locatable sequences' of events such as flashes or bangs,

> Thus a directly locatable sequence of bangs for a speaker-hearer pair at a certain time would be a series of bangs which was going on at that time, or had just ceased at that time, and all the members of which were audible to both members of the pair. So long as the range of reference was understood as restricted within the limits of the series, every member of the series could be identified. . .without reference to any particular of a type other than its own. (*ibid.* p. 37)

The shortcoming of this kind of framework for human use is that it requires 'artificially favourable' circumstances.

> . . .not all flashes and bangs that may be identifying referred to are, on the occasion of the reference, members of a directly locatable sequence for those who refer to them.
> In practice, when we wish to refer identifyingly to a particular phenomenon of this kind, and are not in the artifically favourable position of being able to do so by placing it in a directly locatable sequence, we do so by way of reference,. . .to a particular of some quite different sort. . .(*ibid.* pp. 37-8)

In practice we rely on places and material objects, but as Strawson acknowledges this may reflect only 'a contingent limitation of the human condition' (p. 37). Nevertheless, given our condition, any attempt to base a framework on directly locatable sequences would suffer from 'severe practical limitations' (p. 39).

It is instructive to see how well this framework would serve outside the human condition. In addition to making clear what can and cannot be achieved using it, this will give us an opportunity to begin to develop our model of an immobile language community. So consider not one but a group of feature Placers each rooted in one spot, a community of sentient trees, and let us ask what more is required for these trees to use the abilities they already have, as feature Placers, to communicate with one another.

The phrase, 'what more is required' invites accounts of two quite distinct matters. Obviously these feature Placing trees will require new abilities. They will, for example, each need to be able to distinguish parts of their experience as reports coming in from other members of the group. This is not an ability which should be taken for granted, but it does not fall within the scope of this monograph either to give an account of it or of its acquisition. What we are after here is an account of the ability to collate incoming reports and relate them to the interpreter's own experience. To simplify matters it will be assumed that every member of the group issues reports which bear some recognizable peculiar characteristic, e.g. each member has a recognizable voice. This will give the community a sufficient hold on the identity of 'persons' for us to proceed without needing to confront the philosophical problems which evidently lurk here.

Apart from the new abilities our trees require, we must also pay some attention to the character of their experience. We might, for example, assume that every member of the community has the same experience (same features in the same relations at the same time). This would make it possible for them to use Strawson's directly locatable sequences for every sequence of features would be directly locatable. The trouble with this assumption is that it makes communication pointless. No member of the community would have anything to tell any other member which the other member had not already experienced.

The opposite extreme, no tree has experience which resembles the experience of any other tree for any significant length of time, would make the use of directly locatable sequences rare if not impossible. It might also be thought to make communication as pointless as when every member has the same content to his experience. But it is possible to imagine a tree gaining some advantage from tuning into the chatter of his comrades even when the pattern of their experience never matches his. N might have discovered that when M reports ϕ, N is likely to experience ϕ

before long and ϕ might be something for which he has to prepare the disposition of his organs in order to derive benefit or avoid discomfort. If M is the only other tree whose experience presages his own, paying attention to other reports will have, at most, entertainment value. If, however, many members of his community make reports which have a probable bearing on his future experience he might find himself faced with a traffic problem. A number of possibly useful reports might arrive at once and all or most might be lost because he is able to concentrate on only one at a time. (This is evidently a psychological limitation which afflicts the human condition as well.) If members of the community avoid a useless babble by speaking in turn, a gap may open between the time at which a report is issued and the time to which it applies. A feature Placer receiving a report can associate no Time with a report other than the Time distinguished by his reception of the report, but in timing his response to the situation which a report presages, it may be vital to know the Time to which the report applies. We have here an example of what Strawson might call a 'severe practical limitation'.

What is required to overcome this limitation is a system of dating reports. Such a system will not be available unless the experience of the community has a certain character. Strawson notes that the sequence of nights and days would serve us as a directly locatable sequence, but while acknowledging, 'It is no accident that our dating system makes use of such convenient phenomena' (p. 38) he dismisses it as a 'special and dubious case' (pp. 38-9). It is hard to see what is special or dubious about this; putting the device at the disposal of our sentient trees seems to overcome the problem just outlined.

To put the matter in feature Placer terms: suppose the whole community experiences a pervasive temporal pattern feature, x. ('Pervasive' means no Time fails to overlap a $T(x)$.) The community can establish this is a common directly locatable sequence by enumerating its periods, the individual $T(x)$s, in unison. Reports can now be dated by means of the $\subseteq$ relation between Times. One tree can date an experience of feature ϕ by relating the Time of the experience, say it is the ith experience of ϕ, to the appropriate $T(x)$, thus $T(\phi)_i \subseteq T(x)_j$. (If $T(\phi)_i$ overlaps more than one $T(x)$, the report might be '$T(\phi)_i \subseteq$ Fu $\{T(x)_j : j \; \varepsilon \; J\}$'.) A receiver of this report does not need to be able directly to locate $T(\phi)$s with the sender of the report. The information he receives can evidently be related to his own experience and may help him to time his own responses to his environment.

The only respect in which this system might be dubious is if the periods marked out by the x-feature provide a temporal grid which is too coarse. If one thinks in human terms, knowing the day a thing happened might be insufficient information to time a response to whatever it is that such a thing presages. But to establish that a purely temporal framework might work, we can assume that no feature Placer needs to know the date of a report more accurately than during which $T(x)$s it applies. This would, perhaps, amount to a special assumption. Nature did not provide human beings with a fine enough temporal grid; we were forced to invent clocks. (Is this the contingency which limits human beings and prevents them from using a purely temporal framework?)

If our forest community make use of a dating system, they have a unified temporal framework. Insofar as they are feature Placers with a grasp of the identity of Places they have spatial notions, but nothing so far said requires them to co-ordinate their reports in such a way as to make use of spatial relations between what individual trees experience. They have, in effect, a public time and private spaces. Is there anything vital missing from their framework or their experience?

As so far described, not a great deal of identifying reference takes place in the forest. They have one directly identifiable sequence provided by the x-feature, but everything else that happens is as private as their individual spaces. A feature ϕ does not distinguish the same Times for one tree as it does for another, but perhaps the assumption that allows them only one sequence they can directly identify is overly restrictive. It may be that, during a certain period, ϕ provides a directly locatable sequence for a subgroup; (imagine a sequence of flashes visible in only one part of the forest). What establishes that this subgroup experiences the same sequence is, once again, their ability to count in unison. There is, of course, no possibility that they might recognize that one part of the subgroup experiences a different, but simultaneous, sequence of flashes from the other, but this fact, if they could recognize it, might have no interest for them. Nothing, so far, seems to be missing which would make communication impossible.

Strawson points to a link between the unity of the spatio-temporal framework and *our* concept of reality. If someone tells us a story in which the things and events reported cannot, by the teller's own admission, be related to our own time and place, we take him to be admitting the things spoken of did not *really* exist, the events reported did not *really* happen (1963, pp. 17-18). One sure sign that Tolkein's Ring-cycle is fiction and not history is that no one can relate Middle Earth to Europe or say how long before or after the Thirty Years' War the Wars of the Ring took place. This is where the unity of the framework makes contact with the notion of identifying reference. It is the hearer's ability to relate a report to his own time and place which distinguishes identification proper from story-relative identification.

But how much unity does the framework require? Must a hearer be able to relate what he hears both to his own time *and* to his own place? One might point out that listeners to the Archers can say roughly when events in Ambridge happen in relation to events in their own lives and argue that it is because Ambridge cannot be related with sufficient precision to Cambridge and Uxbridge that we say the events in Ambridge do not *really* happen. But this situation is not analogous to that which obtains in our forest. One tree listens to another in hope of anticipating his own experience. Only the seriously deluded are on the look out when they hear that Dan Archer has lost a prize calf. The situation in the forest is rather like the fantasy in which we exchange radio messages with a station we cannot locate and which describes a world completely unlike ours in geography and politics, but events described as happening in this unlocatable world (earthquakes, famines) strangely anticipate similar events in our own world.

There are a number of avenues by which one might attack either this fantasy or the claim that the picture of the feature Placing forest is coherent. How do we establish a common language with this mysterious radio-station? How do feature Placing trees acquire their language? Are these perhaps not cases of what is no more than fiction functioning as an oracle, and can there be genuine two-way communication either with fiction or with an oracle? Can there be real communication between parties who can check *none* of each other's reports? (There is, of course, communication between parties which cannot check *all* of each other's reports.)

It is unlikely that Strawson's response to this example of a framework unified in time only would be to hunt down one of these avenues for a way of undermining the example. His concern is always explicitly with the *human* situation and aspects of that situation which 'radically condition the nature of identifying reference' (p. 39). The language of the forest might well count as including identifying reference and a concept of reality,

> But this is not to say that our concept [of reality] might not have been different, had the nature of our experience been fundamentally different.
> (1963, p. 18)

The forest of feature Placers evidently do not have our concept of reality because their experience is so different from ours. But what kind of constraint is supposed to make it impossible for us to operate within a framework which is not spatially unified?

The argument against *our* using a purely temporal framework seems to boil down to this: our experience being what it is, we have hit upon a system of identifying reference which uses a framework unified spatially as well as temporally. This enables us to do certain things (refer in certain ways) which we could not if the framework were not so unified. Since it is impossible to do these things without a unified spatial framework and we find it impossible not to want to be able to do them, we find it impossible to do without a unified spatial framework. To think of giving up the purposes served by our unified spatial framework is to think of an experience radically different from the one we have.

Whether this argument accomplishes very much I leave to the judgement of those who are pursuing other problems. There is only one comment which needs to be made here. If, among those things for which we use our spatial framework, Strawson would include the co-ordination of action and experience in finding our way about the world, then he cannot maintain that the framework requires only places and place occupiers (material bodies) for its basic particulars. For we saw above that to use the framework for this requires a grasp of the movements, the possibility of redescribing them in terms of their parts (Section 12). If our mobility is one of the aspects of the human condition which 'radically conditions the nature of identifying reference', then Strawson cannot keep events or processes out of his list of basic particulars.

Trying to imagine how things might be if we did not move about is, indeed, trying to imagine an experience very different from the one we have. If identifying reference is to be possible in such an experience it may not be necessary that the framework used be spatially as well as temporally unified. But Strawson must regard it as at least *possible* for creatures who have this experience to operate with 'just that conception of a single unified framework which we possess'. They must, moreover, be able to do so without making use of principles of identity for events or processes. So our next task is to see if the trees in our forest can put their private spaces together in a single spatial framework.

Section 14

A community whose members did not conceive of changes in their own positions could have a partially unified space if they could establish that members had overlapping viewpoints. This is not a satisfactorily unified space.

As a feature Placer, each member of the forest community is able to distinguish, within his own perceptual field, Places, their limits and extent, their interior and frontier parts. Each tree also has a principle for saying whether two Place encounters, $P(\phi)_i$ and $P(\phi)_j$ are encounters with the same Place. For a single tree, distinct encounters determine Times, but two trees M and N might discover, using the community's dating system, that they each encountered a $P(\phi)$ during the same Time and by exchanging information about the parts of their $P(\phi)$s, determined by the disposition of features within their respective experiences, come to the conclusion that their encounters were encounters with the same Place.

If this is a relatively isolated agreement in their experiences, there is no basis whatever for using this identification of Place to represent what happens when two people discover they experience the same object at the same time. The feature Placers lack a grasp of the vital distinction between occasions like these when they experience the same object and occasions when they experience distinct but similar objects. In spite of lacking this distinction it would be possible for the community to treat implicitly all such cases as though each tree experienced a distinct thing. Because this also introduces the possibility of an unsatisfactory but instructive unification of the private spaces of our community, it is worth pursuing this briefly.

All that is required is an extension of the part/whole relation. When two trees encounter 'the same Place' at the same time they treat these experiences as encounters with distinct parts of a more comprehensive Place which is simply the fusion of all those Places encountered by members of the community who experience that Place at that time. Each tree in effect treats his $P(\phi)$ as distinct from that encountered by any other tree. A natural extension of this device would regard the total Place experienced by a feature Placer at some Time as part of a comprehensive Place which is nothing more than the fusion of Places experienced by the community at that time.

The result *is* a unified space, but one which is unified in only the most facile way. The spatial unity we use when communicating with our fellow humans is not one achieved by simply treating our experience as part of all that is experienced. Our feature Placers remain unable to judge that two of their number are experiencing the same spatial object. Although each feature Placer does make use of a conception of Places which he personally does not experience, the idea of a Place which *no* tree experiences is out of reach—the comprehensive Places are put together out of actually experienced Places; no part of such a Place is not within the purview of some tree or group of trees. There is within this 'unified space' no relationship, between what is experienced by two trees, other than that of being part of the same thing.

There is, indeed, more unity within the space of an individual tree, than there is within that of the whole community. An individual's space may be taken to be connected; this means that the Place which constitutes his field at a given time (the fusion of all Places determined by features within his field) cannot be exhaustively divided into two parts all of whose parts are interior to them, (see above, pp. 52ff.) But the community's space, if unified in the way suggested, will not be a connected space.

To see this, consider a feature Placer before he joins a community of similar creatures. The Place which constitutes his field at a given time is his universe at that time. The boundaries of this Place are not parts of, nor any kind of object within, this Place; there is no distinction between frontier and interior for this Place as a whole. Ax 4 (p. 53, above) specifies that all parts of the universe are interior parts. The reason for this is that for a Place to have a frontier or boundary there must be something outside that Place and there is nothing outside the universe.

But even when the feature Placer comes to accept that he may perceive only part of any Place determined at a *time* by some feature and that therefore there are Places outside those which constitute his field, the Place that constitutes his field acquires neither frontiers nor a boundary. To say which parts of a Place are frontier parts he must be able to say which parts are in contact with Places outside that Place. Merely accepting there are Places other than those in his field does not put him in a position to do this. So the Place which constitutes his field (and hence the field itself) cannot be connected to any Place (or field) outside of itself and each such Place remains a Place all of whose parts are interior parts. The community's space is thus not connected because it can easily be divided exhaustively into parts all of whose parts are interior to them.

From the standpoint of using a spatial framework for identifying reference the most serious shortcoming of this way of unifying the community's space is that it provides no basis for determining when two trees experience the same, as opposed to different, parts of a (the same) Place. Two people may judge they are experiencing the same thing if they know they are looking at the same place. Their judgement that they are looking at the same place is based on a complex co-ordination of a grasp of their own movements through space and how they came to be where they are, together with a grasp of the location and perceptual capacities of the person with whom they are conversing. Their grasp of the identity of place, moreover, depends, as Strawson observed, on a grasp of the identity of bodies. All this looks as though it is inaccessible to a community of immobile feature Placers. They do not think in terms of moving through space and how they came to be where they are; they have no distinction between place and place occupier.

This assessment may be pessimistic, however, only because it is unimaginative. It is not quite true, after all, that there is no distinction between place and place occupier available to our trees. When a feature Placer hears a report of a Place he locates it 'in that other Placer's field'. A place is not *part of* a field; the identity of a perceptual field, unlike the identity of Place, is not tied to features. Why not express the presence of a Place in a field by means of the word 'occupy'? Places are perceptual-field-occupiers. Of course this is not 'occupation' in the sense in which the storage heater occupies a corner of the room. Two people can look at the same corner (and the object occupying it); two feature Placers cannot experience the same perceptual field (and the Place that occupies it). A perceptual field is a logically private object.

Evidently we will have to move the notion of 'perceptual field' away from the category of logically private objects. What might lead us to say that two trees had the same perceptual field (in a loose manner of speaking)? Perhaps if they had the same experience—which they might do if they were planted very close together. The community's basis for accepting that the x-feature, which forms the backbone of their temporal framework, was common experience was their ability to count in unison the periods it distinguished. Suppose two trees discovered that they could count any feature-determined Time-series in unison, that they encountered the same Places at the same Times, that they always reported the same topological relations between Places and Times. In one sense they both experience the same perceptual field. This is not the absurd suggestion that they share a logically unsharable object, but simply a statement about a high degree of conformity between their logically unsharable objects. To mark this sense, let us drop the word 'perceptual' and say these trees 'have the same field'.

If the community is restricted so that every two members have either the same field or completely different fields, it will not be much closer to having a genuinely unified space. From the community's standpoint, two trees which share a field cannot make distinct contributions to the community's conversation. They might as well be regarded as one member with two speaking voices. Unless all the members of the community have the same field (in which case they have nothing to say to each other) the community space remains as disconnected as before.

A more interesting possibility arises if we consider the likely effects of having two trees planted some distance apart. The two might, as a result, share a significant portion of their experience and at the same time each have an important unshared portion of experience. They would thus make distinct contributions to the community's conversation *and* be able to corroborate some of each other's reports. Aided by the stability of certain features in their respective fields each might come to be able to say which of his experiences fall within the other's purview and which do not. One tree might know, for example, that the other cannot perceive beyond the grey (stone) Place into the light green (chervil) Place. Such a reliance on stable features need not be absolute. A (red-brown) fox Place might temporarily blot out both chervil and stone Places, straddling the shared and unshared portion of his field. This tree might be able to predict which fox-part (or incomplete fox-Place) falls in his neighbour's field. Such a feature Placer would in effect have a mastery of an imaginary division of his field—'imaginary' because it is not a division that is or needs to be marked out by the limits of a Place.

Two trees which share some, but not all, of their experience and are able to say with reasonable accuracy which Places at a given time belong also to their partner's experience will be said to have overlapping fields. Before considering the possibility of field-overlap, the suggestion that the members of the community think of their individual spaces, i.e. individual fields, as part of a community space would have given the community space the structure of an atomic model of *CI*. The individual fields would be the atoms of the model; Places within (i.e. which occupy) a field are not parts of that field. When the possibility of field overlap is introduced, an individual tree's field is no longer automatically an atom of the model; any shared portion would be a part of each field; for like the field itself the shared portion does not depend on features or on Places for its identity. To treat the community's space seriously as a mereology, let us extend the term 'field' to apply to overlaps between two or more fields, to portions of a feature Placer's field not shared with another feature Placer and to fusions of two or more fields.

It might be thought that this move cannot be taken, for will it not mean that the identity of a feature Placer's field is dependent on the fields it overlaps? Surely a feature Placer's field remains the field it is, *his* field, regardless of what it overlaps. If perchance two fields which overlapped ceased to overlap, surely both fields would not become different fields? This objection does not take full account of the consequences of moving 'field' away from the category of logically private objects. Fields now depend on feature Placers in the way Places depend on features. To see that the consequence pointed out is reasonable, consider it from this standpoint: if there ceases to be an overlap between two fields, then either one tree has lost part of his field (e.g. through disease) or the two trees have moved apart. Our trees have no conception of their own mobility and no way of saying which of two trees (which once had overlapping viewpoints) has lost part of his field.

Introducing the possibility of field overlap enables some progress to be made toward achieving a connected community space. Once a feature Placer accepts that part of his internally connected field (what was referred to on p. 87 as his 'private space') is part of another self-connected field, he must accept that something in his field is connected to something not in his field and his field thus acquires frontier and boundary. It does not thereby acquire (for the feature Placer) the whole of what we would recognize as its boundary, thinking as we do of the feature Placer as experiencing part of a wider world. Its boundary, for the feature Placer, will be precisely that which divides the overlap region from the rest of his neighbor's field. Two feature Placers M and N whose fields overlap but are connected with no other members of their community each experience part of a single connected field—the fusion of their two fields. But while each of their individual fields thereby acquires a boundary and frontier, they have no basis for thinking of their fusion as having frontier or boundary.

There might, however, be a third tree, L, whose field overlaps M's but not N's. This will provide a boundary within L's field for the field formed by fusing M's and N's fields. The three will together each experience part of a connected field formed by the fusion of all three fields. N's field is not directly connected to L's but may be said to be connected to it via the overlap between N and M and that between M and L. Such connection will be called 'connection by an overlap chain'. Fields may be connected by an overlap chain of any finite number of overlaps.

But unless the whole community is fortunate enough to have every pair of its members connected either directly by an overlap or indirectly by an overlap chain, the community will continue to have a disconnected space. This perhaps needs qualification. It may be possible for two trees to establish that their respective fields are connected but not overlapping. This would be more difficult to imagine than the circumstances that would lead to the recognition of an overlap. But even if this were possible there is still no way for our forest to establish a connected space or connected community field if it consists of groups of trees where members of each group are connected to one another, but the groups are separated by gaps. To connect the community field in such circumstances would require the conception of gaps between fields. N in the paragraph above had to make use of the notion of a gap between his field and L's in order to regard his and L's fields as belonging to a single connected space, but he could do this because M's field filled the gap. As long as the community's space had to be put together from the fields of its members, there is no way to link groups unconnected by an overlap chain.

This is part of a general shortcoming which the present attempt at unifying the community's space shares with the first unsatisfactory attempt made at the beginning of this section. As long as the spatial framework is constituted solely by the fields of members of the community, there will be no 'places' (i.e. fields) which are not within the purview of one or more members of the community. As a result the community has no access to the idea of 'place occupiers' (or field-occupiers, i.e. Places) which exist when not experienced by some member of the community.

Section 15

The community of Section 14 can take Strawson's 'decisive conceptual step'. To apply the distinction attained in taking the step to anything like the extent to which humans apply it, requires the use of a principle of identity for events.

If only limited progress has been made toward connecting the community's space and no progress has been made toward introducing unexperienced Places, considerable progress has, at least, been made toward correcting the most important shortcoming of the original attempt at unification. Taking the step of introducing field overlap opens up the possibility of the community being able to distinguish when two trees experience numerically the same Place and when they experience distinct Places. Quite simply, two trees whose fields overlap, experience the same Place at a given time if it falls within the overlap field. If two trees whose fields are discrete, encounter Places exactly similar in respect of their parts at the same Time, then they encounter distinct Places. Strawson claimed it was a 'decisive conceptual step',

> . . .when the case of 'more cat' or 'cat again' is subdivided into the case of 'another cat' and the case of 'the same cat again'.
>
> (1963, p. 214)

Strawson had in mind subdividing pairs of encounters with cat-features made by one feature placer at different times. But it is surely as decisive a conceptual step when pairs of encounters with cat-features made by two feature-placers at the same time can be so sub-divided.

Once a grasp of this second sub-division has been introduced, the principle by which feature Placers have thus far reidentified Places (above, pp. 71-72) can be replaced by a principle which more closely approximates that which we use when reidentifying bodies. To see how this new principle becomes accessible, consider two trees M and N whose fields overlap and who find a Place, $P(\phi)$, within their overlap at some time. Suppose $P(\phi)$ moves out of the overlap field into that part of M's field which M does not share with N and then after a time moves back into the overlap field. For N this represents two distinct encounters with $P(\phi)$, for M this is a single encounter with $P(\phi)$.

Now with M's help, N can distinguish these two encounters he has had with $P(\phi)$ from the case where, after $P(\phi)$ has left the overlap field and is situated in the unshared part of M's field, ϕ comes to distinguish a further Place in the overlap field similar in every respect to the $P(\phi)$ which still sits in M's field outside the overlap.[3] There are, of course, many situations where N cannot rely on help from M to decide which case (the same or a distinct $P(\phi)$) a pair of encounters represents. But when M *is* able to supply him with a deciding report about the movements of the $P(\phi)$, N *can make* the vital distinction. In a small and limited way, our forest can take the decisive conceptual step Strawson had in mind: subdividing pairs of encounters made by one feature Placer at different times.

Two things need to be noted about the circumstances which permit this step. The identity of a Place or part of a Place must not depend on the field in which it appears. This requires no adjustment to any principle used so far, for Places have depended for their identity only on parts distinguished by features. The other point touches the nerve of this chapter. To supply N with what he needs in order to make the vital distinction between $P(\phi)$ encounters, M has to be able to report the movements of the Place which both trees encounter at the same time. There is no difficulty about reporting movements between fields; field occupations, we just noted, are like topological relations (above, p. 67), they do not affect the identity of Places. But of course the issue is whether in order to transfer the necessary information from M to N, our trees require a grasp of the limits and extent of movements. Do they need to be able to redescribe movements in terms of their parts? Do they require a grasp of a principle of identity for movements?

The basis of N's judgement that he faces the numerically same $P(\phi)$ that he did previously is the unity (which lies in the continuity) of M's observation of that $P(\phi)$ first encountered. To make use of M's report that he has had one encounter with that $P(\phi)$, N must grasp that $P(\phi)$ has moved from one portion of M's field (shared with himself) to another (unshared) portion and back. This information might well be conveyed to N on the level of those reports to transitions between topological relations which are responses requiring no grasp of a principle of identity for transitions or transition States (above, pp. 74-75). One could resist this claim by maintaining that the grasp of the return journey (shared to unshared to shared) requires N to put outward and return journeys together. It would be difficult, however, to push this claim if N and M form an isolated subcommunity (not connected to the rest of the forest); it might be argued that N would need to do this only if he had more complex journeys to keep track of.

There is no need to press the claim that the community would have to be able to redescribe movements in terms of their parts (and hence possess a principle of identity for this kind of event) in order to *take* Strawson's decisive conceptual step. It will easily be seen that this ability is required if the community is to apply the vital distinction between pairs of encounters as widely as we do. Bear in mind that we apply the distinction between *numerically identical* and *similar* not only to encounters made by two people at the same time and encounters made by the same person at different times, but to encounters made by different people at different times. And this latter to encounters made by *any* two people. One can ask for any person X, 'Was the F that X saw at t_1, the same F I saw at t_2?'.

If the sentient forest is to approximate our use of this distinction, N will have to know what it would be to settle the question, 'Is this the same $P(\phi)$ X reported encountering at t_1?' where X is any member of the forest, not just a near neighbor. Suppose that N is connected to J by an overlap chain; that is, N overlaps M, M overlaps L but N does not overlap L, L overlaps K but K does not overlap M, K overlaps J, but J does not overlap L (figure 2).

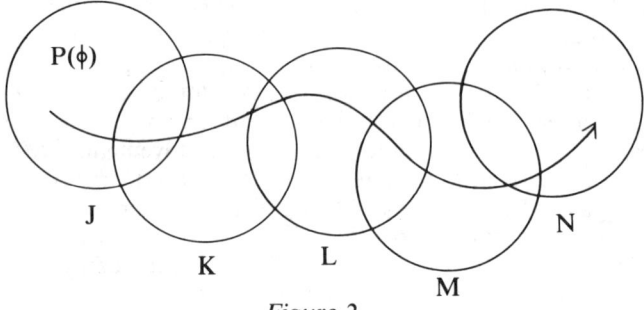

Figure 2

If N is to determine whether the $P(\phi)$ he encounters at t_2 is the same as that which J encountered at t_1, he cannot rely on the continuous encounter with $P(\phi)$ by any one member of his community. No one perceives $P(\phi)$ all the way from J to N, but there are overlapping continuous observations of $P(\phi)$: K oversees the movement from J to L, L from K to M, M from L to N. N can distinguish this case from that where $P(\phi)$ remains parked, say, in K, while another $P(\phi)$ appears in M and moves into N's field. But N can do this only if he can co-ordinate the reports of his fellow trees. The principle of this co-ordination is the journey of $P(\phi)$ from J to N, of which he receives reports of only parts. If he is to answer the question, 'Is this the $P(\phi)$ J encountered?' he has to be able to relate parts of the journey to the whole.[4]

This is one conclusive argument for maintaining that if the forest is to apply the crucial distinction widely enough, it must be able to redescribe movements in terms of their parts. There is a further consideration which reinforces this conclusion. Because we regard the question, 'Was the first

F encountered the same F as the second?' as answerable although no group of people has taken it in turns to keep an eye on the first F encountered, the words, 'in principle' are often incorporated in philosophic formulae to indicate that what *would* have settled the question conclusively is continuous observation or overlapping continuous observations, even where these did not take place.

We can imagine the trees of the sentient forest being in a similar position: N finds he cannot determine whether what he now encounters is what J previously encountered because trees which form the overlap chain(s) between himself and J were inattentive or forgetful, but N can be said to be able to answer the question *in principle* because he knows what information would settle the question and how to use it. But what if there is no overlap chain linking J to N? One might argue that N can still settle the question *in principle* because he knows what it *would* be to be linked to J by an overlap chain. It is important, however, not to forget that N has no access to a conception of unsurveyed fields linking his field to J's. The community's space so far consists only of the fields of its actual members. If N is not in fact linked to $J,$ it is far from clear that he possesses any conception of what would settle the question.

If $P(\phi)$ exits from J's field (or from a field connected to it) and immediately, or after a lapse of time, there appears an exactly similar $P(\phi)$ in N's field (or a field connected to it), the community may decide it was numerically the same $P(\phi)$ in both encounters. But in doing so they are not making use of the principle based on the unity of movements through overlapping continuous observations. (This principle will hereafter be designated by the abbreviation, 'the principle of continuity'.) They do not have the conception necessary if they are to use this principle even to *conjecture* that it might be the same Place. To use the principle of continuity to make this conjecture, they require the idea of unsurveyed fields linking otherwise unconnected fields.

We saw above that—except in the specially favoured situation where every pair of members is linked by an overlap chain—what is required for the community to have a spatial framework with at least the unity that consists in its being connected is a notion of fields which are not surveyed by some member of the community. We have just seen that for the community to apply the principle of continuity as widely as we in fact do (so that one tree can ask, for any fellow tree X, 'Is this the $P(\phi)$ X encountered?') they also require a notion of unsurveyed fields. This makes clear one important connection between the unity of a spatial framework and the use of a principle of reidentification, as well as the connection between these two and the role of unsurveyed regions in a (unified) spatial framework.

What can be said about the grasp of a spatial framework which includes regions not perceived by some members of the community? It is easy enough to say N and J might come to think of themselves as related by an overlap chain whose intermediate fields fall within the experience of possible members (or actual, but dumb, members) of the community. This idea might rest on an analogy with the overlap chains which N and J know to exist between themselves and other actual members of their community. A vague explanation appealing to the community's use of analogy might be sufficient for some purposes, but it is worth pressing here for a more detailed account. What would an immobile community do with such an idea? What in their experience would suggest that such regions exist? Could any precise content be given to the analogy?

In a space as unstructured as that of our sentient forest, there is not a great deal of scope for making the analogy between surveyed and unsurveyed fields precise, but there are relationships between actually connected fields one might hope could be imposed on otherwise unconnected fields as a result of applying the analogy. If N's field is actually connected to the field belonging to L, there are one or more overlap chains linking his field to L's, each with a precise number of members providing the overlapping fields. N has to take account of this if he is to keep track of the movements of a Place between L's field and his own. Since there can be more than one overlap chain linking N to L, some containing more trees than others, these alternative links might suggest to the community more and less direct routes, a rough notion of direction and the idea that some fields lie 'between' N and L because they form parts of the most direct route. If N is to make use of the conception of unperceived fields connecting his field to J's, will anything suggest the direction of the most direct route?. . .whether fields connected to either N or J lie between them along this route?. . .roughly how many trees would be required to make the connection actual?

Before trying to answer this, it is worth trying to imagine what the community could do with the notion of unsurveyed fields and the analogy between them and surveyed fields. What difference could this idea make to the behaviour of creatures who do not move and do not think of themselves as mobile? At least our sentient trees are not totally incapable of action. We have already used the idea that they listen to the reports of their fellows in order to anticipate their own pleasures and discomforts. This they might well improve if they thought of the various disconnected clumps of the forest as parts of a single connected space. The connected containing space with its unperceived regions would act as an explanatory framework. But they might get along without this framework. The appearances of a feature in one connected group might herald the appearance of that feature in another group unconnected to the first, but to anticipate this the second group need not associate the temporal gap between appearances with a spatial gap separating the two fields.

The idea of unperceived places might, however, make a difference to their behaviour if they had control over their propagation and could determine to some extent where on the periphery of various isolated subcommunities they established saplings. In other words, it might make a difference if they could control to some extent the actual space (or actually surveyed space) that they have. Because they could act to effect a connection between otherwise unconnected subgroups and seek to do so as economically as possible, they could make use of the ideas of direct and indirect routes across gaps which divide one subgroup from another. Haphazard propagation might succed in linking subgroups, but it might also take a long time or fail altogether.

Will the experience of population growth serve as an account of the origin of the idea of unsurveyed regions? The community has experienced an increase in the number of fields it surveys, so it imagines there are more regions waiting to be surveyed by new trees? By itself population growth need not suggest that fields are waiting to be explored rather than created by the propagation of the species. But if the propagation can be controlled with the aim of linking two unconnected groups, if decisions have to be taken about locating saplings and estimates have to be made about how many saplings it will take, so there will be correct and incorrect actions to be measured against outcome, the community will have to operate with an idea of the independent existence of unsurveyed regions between unconnected subgroups.

What within the community's experience will guide the estimates and decisions they take? We noted that the only frontiers or boundaries to his own field, which a tree can recognize, are those formed by fields connected to his, and there is within a field which is a maximally connected fusion of fields no automatic way of telling which trees lie on the frontier. There may be ways for a tree to tell whether the whole of, what we would think of as, the boundary of his field is saturated, that is whether a new tree could overlap his field without overlapping the field of another tree already overlapping his field, but we have not considered these and must not take the possibility for granted.

Can a tree tell whether the boundary of his field is saturated? Suppose ϕ is a feature which has a principle of spatial completeness (is a shape or pattern feature) and M recognizes an incomplete ϕ-Place in the overlap field he shares with N, but N assures him that he, N, perceives a complete ϕ-Place, part of which falls in the overlap region. Perhaps other Places in his experience will suggest to *M* that he perceives only part of something of which, as far as he knows, no one perceives the whole. There might, of course, be occasions when the opposite happens. Incomplete ϕ-Places in the overlap field which are simply imcomplete, not partly out of view. When *M* cannot check with *N* or any other tree, what will make him choose the hypothesis he perceives only part of a ϕ-Place rather than that he perceives the whole of an incomplete ϕ-Place?

If Places move into and out of *N*'s field, will they not appear on the boundary of his field? Will this not provide evidence of an unsaturated boundary? Yes, but only if the tree has reason to rule out the possibility of Places suddenly appearing on the interior of his field. Reason for ruling this out might come from the regularity with which Places move across the connected field of the group to which he belongs. It is significant that he would have to co-operate in 'Place-tracking' exercises if he were to have access to this principle.

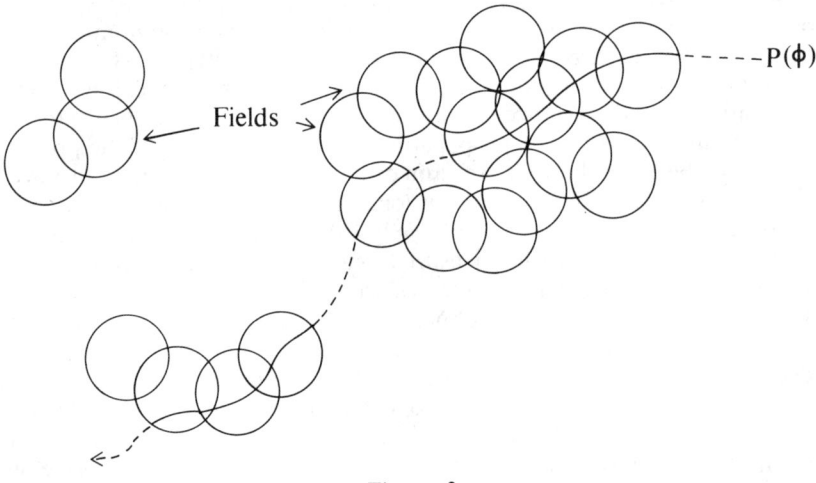

Figure 3

If a tree could tell that his boundary was unsaturated, this might only mean that his group partially or completely surrounds a gap and would not, in any case, provide a way of deciding which unsaturated boundaries should be built onto if his subgroup is to make contact with another group. 'Place-tracking' exercises might, however, suggest the presence of gaps in the midst of a connected group or between unconnected groups. Movements of Places could guide the location of gaps and of other fields in this way: Places moving across a connected subgroup following certain paths might disappear and a similar Place appear within the same group. A high correlation between movements in a certain direction before disappearance and the appearance of a similar Place in another region of the subgroup would, perhaps, suggest that one Place passed through a gap in the midst of the group. A similar high correlation between certain paths in one group and the appearance of exactly similar Places after a lapse of time (Time) in another unconnected group would suggest a gap between the groups *and* along which unsaturated boundaries the groups should extend themselves if they wish to establish a connection.

There appear to be very few resources from which the community could build a unified spatial framework which do not require them to use a grasp of the movements of Places between fields. This would, moreover, have to be a grasp which includes an ability to relate parts of a movement to the whole of the movement, for they must do this if they are successfully to correlate the path a Place takes before vanishing with the appearance of a similar Place (conjectured to be the same Place) in another field. The need for this ability to relate the parts and wholes of movements is even more obvious if we consider what the community must do to make an estimate of the distance in number of trees between unconnected groups.

Suppose that some kinds of Places move through the connected groups of the community along much the same paths with a fair degree of regularity and a velocity sufficiently constant for the community to make estimates in terms of x-periods of how long it will take for a Place to traverse a field. For the sake of illustration, imagine that one kind of Place takes roughly one x-period to cross one field. If the lapse of Time between one of these Places disappearing from one group and a similar Place appearing in another unconnected group were constant, say n x-periods, it would be possible not only to conjecture that it is the same Place which appears in the second group, but to estimate that (roughly) n fields must be established to connect the two groups so that the Places could be kept under surveillance for the whole trip between the groups. This is an estimate which cannot be made without a fairly sophisticated grasp of the divisibility of movements.

In describing what it would be for this immobile community to employ the notion of unsurveyed fields in order to unify its space, we have thus reinforced the conclusion that to apply sufficiently widely the distinction between encounters with similar but distinct objects and encounters with numerically the same object, an immobile community requires a grasp of the identity of movements in terms of part and whole. To apply the distinction as widely as we apply it requires a unified spatial framework, and the unification of that framework rests on an ability to redescribe the movement of place (field) occupiers in terms of their parts. Strawson's position requires it to be possible for a language community such as this to use this distinction and to possess a unified spatial framework without needing a grasp of a principle of identity for events or processes. But it is not possible to use the distinction or to possess the unified framework without an ability to redescribe movements, which amounts to the possession of a principle of identity for events. Strawson's position, that a set of basic particulars need not include events, has thus been shown to be untenable.

Section 16

The preceding eleven sections have established a number of points relevant to any more general theoretical approach to our grasp of identity principles.

The argument against Strawson's position in this Chapter has taken the form of a dilemma (see p. 83): in order to possess a unified framework of reference the members of a linguistic community either must conceive of their own movements within that framework, or they need not. Section 12 argued that if they must then they require principles of identity for particular movements (journeys). Section 15 completed the argument by showing that if they need not conceive of their own movements within the framework, they still require such principles. In both sections the argument rested on the principle that the ability to redescribe a movement in terms of its parts constituted the grasp of a principle of identity.

Resistance to the use of this principle was anticipated at the end of Section 9 and there it was argued (p. 64f) that where, in addition to redescribing wholes in terms of their parts, judgements involving the topological relations of Section 8 were also made, we could confidently say the concepts of part and whole were being used strictly rather than metaphorically. In each of the applications of the principle in this chapter it can be seen that such topological relations are not only available but are integral to the judgements which ensure the unity of the space. It is clear that in each case the topological relations were involved in the structure of the paths followed (by the language users themselves in Section 12 and by Places in Section 15) and there is a natural homeomorphism between the part-whole and topological structure of a path and the movements along that path. Nor is it sufficient in either case for the language user to redescribe only the path in terms of its parts; in each case he must be able to discuss with his fellows different journeys of the same thing along the same path.

Section 9, however, acknowledged that resistance to the claim that we are here dealing with genuine identity judgements is not rooted only in the suspicion that the argument rests on a metaphorical use of part and whole. The resistance may also rest on a less precise feeling that more is needed to establish the need for or presence of genuine judgements of identity. The feeling must be described as less precise because the notion of a 'genuine' identity judgement (and behind it the notion of a 'genuine' object) is exceedingly vague.

As soon as the feature Placer was equipped to use sentences with quantifier complexity (Section 6, p. 44) he could, by a widely accepted doctrine of ontological commitment, be credited with the possession of a principle for making genuine identity judgements. Resistance which is untouched by this observation, more than likely has its roots in a prejudice in favour of the material object paradigm; but resistance which is too deeply rooted in prejudice can turn out to be philosophically uninteresting. So long as any difference can be pointed to between the putative objects of some category and pieces of furniture, it will be claimed that the putative objects do not enter *genuine* identity judgements. But it would be madness to argue that there are no differences between a journey and a piece of furniture. The interesting questions turn on the place which both putative and undeniable objects have in the logical structure of our discourse.

There is nevertheless an important worry which it is reasonable to express by using the word 'genuine', which does not boil down to materialist prejudice, and which is not answered by pointing to the possibility of using sentences with quantifier complexity. There is a clear sense in which the feature Placer of Sections 6-8 has an ontology radically different from our own and in which the community of Section 15, in spite of their immobility, have an ontology very much nearer to ours. In this sense it would be fair to say that possibly the latter and certainly not the former could be claimed to have genuine identity principles. Indeed, it has been the aim of this monograph to develop theoretical machinery which would make that sense plainer.

The worry arises because the same principle of identity is seen to work in both places. Surely if a grasp of the identity principle which permits redescription in terms of parts can leave one with the bizzare ontology of Sections 6-8, it cannot guarantee 'genuine' identity judgements. After all, it left the objects of that ontology 'insufficiently particular'.

This worry stems from a misunderstanding of the theoretical load which principles of identity can, and have here been required to, carry—a misunderstanding which it has been in part the aim of this monograph to expose and combat. It would (in the light of the second two chapters) be ridiculous to claim that pointing out how it is possible for journeys to be redescribed in terms of their parts provides by itself an adequate theoretical account of the mastery of the identity of such objects. The forest community's ability to redescribe journeys clearly rests on (among other things) the identity of members of the community and the ability to distinguish Place-encounters. It has been no part of my claims in this monograph that an account of the principles by which objects can be redescribed provides by itself a sufficient account of the mastery of such principles—indeed the aim is to suggest that it is only in the context of a more general account of what language users must be able to do that such principles shed any light at all.

The monograph has treated our own mastery of identity principles largely by contrast with artificial models of language users. A direct treatment is well beyond the scope of a monograph of this size but the theoretical machinery which was constructed in order to clarify and test Strawson's position has unearthed important points which would have to be treated in any thorough account of our own mastery of the identity of the objects in the various categories we possess.

(1) From Section 5 it is clear that identity principles must, if nothing else, equip those who use them to apply more than one word or phrase to a single thing, and conversely where this is possible we may look for the mastery of identity principles.

(2) One way to display the mastery of the identity of something is to be able to discuss its limits and extent. There are precise logical and mathematical tools which help to clarify that ability (Sections 6 and 8) but such tools do not as yet give a complete account of all elements of that mastery; in particular they do not reflect what Section 9 called principles of completeness.

(3) The abilities mentioned under (1) and (2), even in combination are not sufficient to enable a language user to make the distinctions required for reidentifying those particulars we are accustomed to think of as paradigm objects. It took not only logical improvement in the means available for making temporal discrimination, but also the ability to count, in order to guarantee the possibility of making the required distinctions. Whether this is the only way to guarantee this possibility is a question which will need to be treated by any more general theory.

(4) The distinction which amounted to that between place and place occupier (viz. *Place* and *field* in Section 14) rested in part on a grasp of the identity of other members of the language community. Whether this is the only way to achieve this distinction is another thing which should be considered in any more general theoretical approach to identity. If one approaches the structure of a perceptual field via the apparatus of CI and takes seriously the problems considered in Section 7 there does seem to be a *prima facie* doubt that a solipsistic consciousness could have access to anything amounting the distinction between place and place occupier.

(5) The 'decisive conceptual step' (p. 96) of distinguishing pairs of encounters with Xs by one language user at different times into 'encounters with the same X' and 'encounters with different Xs' has a complement whose importance is frequently overlooked. It is equally decisive when two encounters of Xs by different language users at the same time can be divided into 'encounters with the same X' and 'encounters with different Xs'.

It remains only to reflect briefly on the relation beween the conclusions reached here and the theoretical aims which were pursued.

Michael Dummett has advanced the thesis that in seeking a theory of meaning we are or should be seeking a 'theoretical representation of a practical ability' (1976, p. 69). Taken without further elaboration, that phrase captures the spirit of the present investigation. The aim throughout has been to understand our practice, if only by trying to imagine an alternative practice. Language use has been treated as involving a complex ability which the user successfully exhibits without necessarily understanding how he succeeds. An attempt was made to represent that complex ability by gradually adding to a set of simpler abilities and at each stage questions about differences in ability were answered in terms of differences in manifestation.

I would hesitate, however, to claim to have written an essay in the theory of meaning as Dummett understands the enterprise, for I am far from confident I can anticipate what he would count as satisfying the description, a 'theoretical representation of a practical ability'. Dummett's writings within the area covered in this investigation do not present themselves as constituting anything like a finished theory, but a number of theses for which Dummett warmly argues have been implicitly endorsed by the way the theoretical apparatus of this monograph was developed.

The most central thesis to be found in Dummett's treatment of identity is the Frege-Wittgenstein principle that 'with a name must be associated a criterion of identity' (1973, p. 73). I have eschewed the word 'criterion' in favour of 'principle' since Section 2, because I did not want to suggest the possession of something consciously employed. But this appears to conform to Dummett's conception of a criterion for he writes,

> In these terms, what someone who knows the proposition expressed by a sentence containing a proper name must have is not . . . familiarity with a particular way of picking out or identifying the object, but simply an ability to recognise it when presented with it. We must not ask *how* or *by what* the object is recognised; even if there is an answer the subject does not have to know it.
>
> (1978, p. 129)

For Dummett the key to object-status is the possibility of applying predicates to the putative object (1973, p. 79). Without this possibility no distinction can be made between noun and adjective, singular term and predicate (*ibid.*, p. 78). This thesis is close to the point frequently emphasized here that a principle of identity enables several words or phrases to be applied to the same thing.

Dummett also maintains that 'the criterion of identity is not derivable

from the criterion of application' (1973, p. 74). From the point at which
the feature placer was replaced by the feature Placer, it was clear that the
grasp of any principles of identity required more than the ability to
produce the right sign in the appropriate circumstances. The point is
made here in terms quite different from the argument Dummett uses (he
relies on the possibility of one word 'book' having two senses, 'copy' and
'literary work' whose difference cannot be explained in terms of criteria
of application) and this serves to reinforce his position.

Finally, any approach to the meaning of singular terms which inquires
into a speaker's *mastery* of his language will have to recognize some kind
of distinction between the *sense* of such an expression (what he understands when he knows what that expression means) and the *object* to
which the expression refers. Under such an approach Mill's doctrine that
'the linguistic function of a proper name consists in a direct association
between the name and the object, of which no further account can be
given' will have no attraction whatsoever (1978, p. 128). In this
monograph the use of a singular term of any kind was represented as
resting on a complex of abilities which included the ability to respond
correctly to the appropriate environmental circumstances and made no
use of a direct unanalysable relation between singular term and the
object to which it refers. I am convinced that this is the correct way for
theory to treat the relation between referring expression and referent as
well as the correct way to represent the relation between singular term
and predicate, and this conviction arises out of my understanding of the
aims of a philosophic theory of language.

Notes

CHAPTER 1

1 'Event' is not necessarily the same as 'change': 'It seems likely to me that the concept of an event depends in every case on the idea of a change in a substance, despite the fact that for some events it is not easy to say what substance it is that undergoes the change' (Davidson 1970, p. 226). Crucial for what follows is the uncertain relation which 'event' bears to a whole host of items; as Davidson says 'The theory under discussion is silent about processes, states and attributes if these differ from individual events' (1971, p. 82).

2 In the original article the criterion was printed incorrectly, with conditionals on the right side.

3 'Perhaps sameness of causal relations is the only condition always sufficient to establish sameness of events (sameness of location in space and time may be another)' (1970, p. 231). The suggestion in parenthesis leaves us in the dark about how events are to be distinguished from material bodies.

4 'The principle of the nomological character of causality must be read carefully: it says that when events are related as cause and effect, they have descriptions that instantiate a law. It does not say that every true singular statement of causality instantiates a law' (1971, p. 89). In particular, Davidson holds that there are no laws relating mental and physical event descriptions (*ibid.*, p. 81 and *passim*). This means that no creature could apply Davison's criterion to establish his further thesis that a mental event can sometimes be redescribed as a physical one (*ibid.*, pp. 81, 99-101). The coherence of his overall position requires a strongly realist attitude to events (see next paragraph) but the criterion can do nothing to support this attitude.

5 Notes of a Balliol College reading party (September, 1972 shown to me by Dr A J Kenny) at which Davidson was present, show him reluctant to include states among events, although in print (e.g. above, n. 1) he is cagey about the matter. It also appears that 'cause' for Davidson holds only between events, which means that our intuitions about the grammar of 'cause' cannot be used to determine what counts as an event description.

6 Justification for associating Strawson with the second thesis comes from the ease with which it seems 'we can frame the idea of another particular bound to the first by the attributive tie'. There seems to be no more to 'framing the idea' than there is to grasping a grammatical transformation rule and coupling the result with adjectives. For further justification, see note 11 to the present chapter.

7 Even within the spirit in which Martin and Taylor offered their analyses, it may not be taken without question that periods and instants of time are less obscure than events. If one's standards of conceptual clarity and primitiveness are not dictated by an attempt to account for our grasp of our native language, they are likely to be dictated by considerations relevant to the foundations of theoretical physics, and here it is also a contentious matter whether times can be taken as more clear or fundamental than events.

8 Most of the arguments Goldman directs against Davidson's identity thesis (1970, pp. 1-4) are addressed to this and similar examples of event identity.

9 There does seem to be a bias against thinking of events as complex in Davidson's proposed identity criterion. The causal network lacks a way of reflecting the part-whole relation. Causes and effects are said to succeed one another. But if events form complexes, the identity of such complexes would be tied as much to their constituents as to their causal relatives.

10 It may be worth dignifying the different answers to 'How long does it take to ϕ?' by speaking of the intensive and extensive durations of ϕing. The terminology is adapted from Sanford (1967, pp. 329-30) who distinguishes the intensive volume of a container — the volume of its walls, bottom and top — from the extensive volume — the intensive volume plus capacity.

11 It is Strawson's silence on these points that in part justifies associating his position with thesis (2). 'Is wise' may be seen in this light as an unfortunate example in that there are no principles for distinguishing instances of wisdom which are not closely tied to principles for distinguishing persons. To associate 'Carr's catch' and 'the blow Peter gave John' with 'Socrates' wisdom' disguises the fact that the grasp of the first two attributive singular terms may depend on more than being able to individuate persons.

CHAPTER 2

1 This argument may be reinforced by considering the picture Quine draws of two possible confusions into which a child might fall over the plural of 'apple'. '[The Child] has really got on to divided reference, one is tempted to suppose, once he responds with the plural 'apples' to a heap of apples. But not so. He may at that point have learned 'apples' as another mass term, applicable to just so much apple as is taken up in apple heaps. 'Apples', for him, would be subordinated to 'apple' as is 'warm water' to 'water' and 'bright red' to 'red'. '. . .We might well not detect, for a while, his misconception: that '-s' just turns mass terms into more specialized mass terms connoting clumpiness.

'A plausible variant misconception is this: 'apple' masswise might cover not apples generally, but just lone ones, while 'apples' still figures as last suggested. Then apples and apple would be mutually exclusive rather than subordinate the one to the other.'   (1960, p. 93)

2 Strawson (1963, p. 212) explicitly disavows any intention to present a model of human language acquisition. Quine, on the other hand, seems content to use similar considerations to contribute to a genetic model (1960, Chapter 2.)

3 The feature placer thus equipped with propositional connectives is, for all the demands Quine makes on an informant, not easily distinguished from the native speaker in Quine's picture of the situation of radical translation.

4 Strawson elsewhere acknowledges that particulars collect 'universals' or 'general characteristics' (1963, pp. 168-182; 1971, pp. 101-15), but he does not use the model of a feature placing language to highlight the importance of this, nor does he to my knowledge associate the grasp of this with a grasp of principles of identity.

5 Strawson concentrates his discussion on places and space, giving hardly any attention to time.

6 'Terms' is the word he actually used: 'In an elementary proposition we can distinguish one or more *terms* from one or more *concepts*; the *terms* are whatever can be regarded as the *subject* of the proposition, while the concepts are the predicates or relations asserted on these terms. The terms of elementary propositions we will call individuals; these form the first or lowest type.

'It is unnecessary, in practice, to know what objects belong to the lowest type, or even whether the lowest type of variable occurring in a given context is that of individuals or some other. For in practice only the *relative* types of variables are relevant; thus the lowest type occurring in a given context may be called that of individuals, so far as that context is concerned.'   (Russell 1967, p. 164)

7 As they acknowledged (p. 46) their calculus closely followed Lesniewski's Mereology. On Lesniewski's work, see Sobocinski, 1954.

8 Where Strawson pictures the syntax of a feature-Placing language by 'It ϕs p, t', I am suggesting the syntax should look more like 'P(ϕ) $\subseteq$ P(ψ) & T(ϕ) $\subseteq$ T(χ)', (although Places and Times *can* be specified by means of more than one feature). This corresponds to the second and less favoured of two possible interpretations which Strawson considers for 'It ϕs p, t' (*op. cit.,* pp. 225-6), according to which feature words may be applied to any part of a Place to which they may be applied, rather than (favoured interpretation) to only the whole Place. Conforming to the favoured interpretation would cut the feature Placer off from any display of his grasp of the limits and extent of the Place determined by a feature. Note that it is possible to conform to this interpretation (less favoured by Strawson) and still accept the consequences of the convention (above, p. 32) that a feature Placer reports 'cat' only when confronting at least one whole cat, viz. that the feature Placer treats the cat-Place as extending only over the complete cat-shapes in his experience. Nothing prevents him from distinguishing parts of this Place and reporting that these parts 'are cat', i.e. parts of the cat-Place.

9 This claim is similar to that which can be made vis-à-vis numbers: providing one has a grasp of the operations of placing sets in one-one correspondence one can determine whether the number of cats is greater than the number of dogs without presupposing a grasp of the criterion of identity for numbers, indeed without presupposing even the ability to recite the numerals in their proper order.

10 Setting aside the examples (1963, 4a19-22) which make clear what Aristotle had in mind, his formula 'what is numerically one and the same is able to receive contraries' (a10-11) fits Places and Times in that they are able to 'receive contraries' in different parts.

11 Whitehead is the only philosopher or mathematician I have discovered who felt it worthwhile to attempt anything like a project of this sort. In 1920, p. 76

'connectedness' is called 'junction'; the two definitions offered there only work if it is assumed that all 'events' (the 'Individuals' of Whitehead's theory) are self-connected. This assumption cannot be made here if we are to use the relation of 'connectedness' to define self-connectedness. (The account of 'interior' which follows below applies equally to non-self-connected Individuals.) In 1960, pp. 449-454 neither of these definitions is used; 'connection' is taken as a primitive notion, but Whitehead's 'assumptions' give only the scantiest account of its properties.

12 To deny these are semantic powers is to limit the interest of semantics. One may choose to concern oneself only with the powers of a physical mixture which can be traced directly to the power of some constituent, but this is completely to ignore the phenomena which interest a chemist.

13 Quine (1960, p, 175): 'The internal structure of these recalcitrant compounds is, relative to canonical notation, just not structure.' Compare Davidson, 1967a p. 82 and Taylor 1974, pp. 113-5.

14 According to Kenny 1963, p. 67 the concept of fear 'stands on three struts', fearful circumstances, symptoms of fear, action taken to avoid what is feared.

15 To represent the use of topological marks (in a manner uniform with that used above for feature marks) will require using fragments of sentences reporting topological relations, e.g. 'c P(green)' to fill the place in 'P(/)' reserved for the mark, e.g. 'P(c P(green)/cats)' for the part of P(cats) which constitute complete cat-shapes and touch the green (felt).

16 In the degenerate case where the only resource is a single word series, '1', this procedure generates the series at which Turing Machines are adept:

1, 11, 111, 1111, . . .

CHAPTER 3

1Transition States should not be taken as models of movements or processes. The feature Placer lacks something necessary for a grasp of the distinction between those parts of a transition State during which something happened and those during which nothing happened. To grasp this he would need a means of comparing the extent to which A is in contact with B, e.g. he would have to be able to distinguish between half and a third of A's boundary being determined by contact with B.

2 I take it that, '. . .the fundamental condition of identification without dependence on alien types—viz. the forming of a comprehensive and sufficiently complex type-homogeneous framework of reference' (1963, p. 45) does not rule out a framework of bodies *and* places so long as, from their mutual dependence, bodies and places are reckoned to be of the same type.

3 For a discussion of the principles by which M might distinguish the two Places ϕ determines in his field, see pp. 66-67.

4 Moreover, unless he can do this he will not be able to apply the distinction to pairs of his own encounters at all widely. For a $P(\phi)$ N encounters at one time may well journey as far as J before returning to N's field.

Index of Initial Occurrences

of words and symbols which are used for technical purposes in this monograph.

Note: ordinary words borrowed for technical purposes are in some cases marked by an initial capital letter.

Bibliography

Anscombe, G E M 1964, 'Substance', *Proceedings of the Aristotelian Society, Supplementary Volume* 38 (1964) 69–78

Aristotle, 1963, *Categories and de Interpretatione,* translated by J L Ackrill, Clarendon Press, 1963

Austin, J L 1962, *Sense and Sensibilia,* Clarendon Press

Benacerraf, P 1965, 'What Numbers Could Not Be', *Philosophical Review* 74 (1965) 47–73

Broad, C D 1923, *Scientific Thought,* Kegan Paul

Burge, Tyler 1972, 'Truth and Mass Terms', *Journal of Philosophy* 69 (1972) 263–82

Cartwright, Helen M 1965, 'Heraclitus and the Bath Water', *Philosophical Review* 74 (1965) 466-85

Davidson, Donald 1967a, 'The Logical Form of Action Sentences', in Rescher N (ed.), *The Logic of Decision and Action,* University of Pittsburgh Press, 81–120

1967b, 'Causal Relations', *Journal of Philosophy* 64 (1967) 691–703

1968, 'Actions, Reasons and Causes', in White, A (ed.), *Philosophy of Action,* Oxford University Press

1970, 'The Individuation of Events', in Rescher, N (ed.), *Essays in Honour of Carl Hempel,* D Reidel, 216-34

1971, 'Mental Events', in Foster, L and Swanson, J, *Experience and Theory,* Belknap Press, 79–101

Dedekind, R 1963, *Essays on the Theory of Numbers,* Dover Press

Dummett, Michael 1973, *Frege—the Philosophy of Language,* Duckworth.

1976, 'What is a Theory of Meaning (II)?', in Evans, G and McDowell, J (eds.) *Truth and Meaning,* Oxford University Press

1978, *Truth and Other Enigmas,* Duckworth

Frege, Gottlob 1950, *The Foundations of Arithmetic,* translated by Austin, J L, Basil Blackwell

1964, *The Basic Laws of Arithmetic,* translated by Furth, M, University of California Press

Geach, P T 1969, God and the Soul, Routledge and Kegan Paul

Goldman A I 1970, *A Theory of Human Action,* Prentice Hall

Goodman, N 1966, *The Structure of Appearance,* 2nd edition, Bobbs-Merrill

Kenny, A J P 1963, *Action, Emotion and Will,* Routledge and Kegan Paul

Lacey, A R 1976 *A Dictionary of Philosophy,* Routledge and Kegan Paul

Leonard, H S and **Goodman, Nelson** 1940 'The Calculus of Individuals and its Uses', *Journal of Symbolic Logic* 5 (1940) 45-55.

Lyons, J 1968, *Introduction to Theoretical Linguistics,* Cambridge University Press

Martin, R M 1969, 'On Events and Event Descriptions', in Margolis, J (ed.), *Fact and Existence, Basil Blackwell,* 63-109

Mendelson, B 1962, Introduction to Topology, Allyn and Bacon.

Moravcsik, J M E 1968, 'Strawson and Ontological Priority', in Butler, R J (ed.) *Analytical Philosophy,* (Second Series), Basil Blackwell, 106-19

Quine, W V 1960, *Word and Object,* M I T Press

Russell, Bertrand 1967, 'Mathematical Logic as Based on the Theory of Types' in van Heijenoort, J (ed.), *From Frege to Gödel,* Harvard University Press

Sanford, D 1967, 'Volume and Solidity', *Australasian Journal of Philosophy,* 45 (1967) 329-39

Sobocinski, B 1954, 'Studies in Lesniewski's Mereology', *Polski Towarzystwo Naukowe Na Obezynie* 5 (1954-5) 34-43

Strawson, P F 1963, *Individuals,* Doubleday (Anchor).

1971, *Logico-Linguistic Papers,* Methuen

Taylor, B 1974, *The Semantics of Adverbs,* Oxford, D.Phil Thesis, Bodleian Library

Thalberg, Irving 1971, 'Singling out Actions, Their Properties and Components', *Journal of Philosophy,* 68 (1971) 781-7

Thomson, Judith J 1971, 'The Time of a Killing', *Journal of Philosophy* 68 (1971) 115-32.

Tiles, J E 1976, 'Davidson's Criterion of Event Identity', *Analysis,* 36 (1976) 185-7

Tiles, M E 1974, *Matter, Motion and the Individuation of Material Bodies,* Oxford B.Phil, Thesis, Bodleian Library

van Fraassen, Bas C 1970, *An Introduction to the Philosophy of Time and Space,* Random House

Whitehead, A N 1920, *The Concept of Nature,* Cambridge University Press.

1960, *Process and Reality,* Harper and Row.